In memory of my father, the late great Robert Charles Elwell, and my wonderful mother Pamela Jayne Elwell.

Bristol born. Quite thoughtful, with a love of life and adventures. A totally original dress sense, a passion for anything on wheels and a talent for bass playing. Blended together with a wicked sense of humour to give the unique and insightful world view of Nathan Robert Elwell.

Nathan Elwell

TRAINS, TRAFFIC JAMS AND OTHER ANNOYANCES

AUSTIN MACAULEY PUBLISHERS™

LONDON • CAMBRIDGE • NEW YORK • SHARJAH

A CIP catalogue record for this title is available from the British
Library.

ISBN 9781528910965 (Paperback)
ISBN 9781786125132 (E-Book)

www.austinmacauley.com

First Published (2018)
Austin Macauley Publishers Ltd.
25 Canada Square
Canary Wharf
London
E14 5LQ

Acknowledgements

I would like to acknowledge the great list of individuals who helped support me and fed and watered me through the years, and encouraged me to turn my mountain of notes into this published piece of literature. Although you are not mentioned in the text itself, you do now feature here in the front of the book.

Alice Moore, Rob Allan, Iain Elwell, Lorna and David Lang, Kev Symonds, the Ratcliff family (Ben, Dan, Sue and Pete), Ellie Denyer, Jo Hurley, Richard and Tom Key of Riks Takeaway.

Special mention has to be made of Laura. A beautiful girl whom I met on a bus back from Bideford to Ilfracombe, and her equally stunning sister, Lucy.

Foreword

"According to statistics published RECENTLY, it has been said that the United Kingdom now has approximately half the length of train track it had during the so-called 'golden age' of the rail industry in the 1930s. Counter to this, the same report explained that the current loading on the rail network as a public transport system sits somewhere in the region of three times as many people traveling on trains now than during the heyday of the transport's social popularity. With these facts in mind, it is unsurprising that even minor problems can cause the occasional bout of complete chaos seen on the network."

— the late Robert Charles Elwell, 2011

Prologue
Traffic Jams

Two questions for you to think about. Question one: can 12 months of a seemingly ordinary series of events become, for better or worse, a life changing year?

Question two: can a mode of transport make or break your day?

During the story to follow I will endeavour to explain my opinions and answers to the above questions, and the reasons why I came to my conclusions. In order to be able to compare transport on an even keel later on, and give my opinions a true sense of context, the background to our story actually begins two years before the main timeline of events that I actually wish to recount in detail. It also begins with the common occurrence of me sitting in the corner of my bedroom manically typing away on my computer while listening to music. Which rather neatly allows me to directly quote Rod Stewart's classic track 'Maggie May': "It's late September and I really should be back at school," in fact, I am patiently awaiting the release of my university timetable for the academic year ahead. This year, however, was to be different from the previous couple; this was the year that my life was about to change completely as I was no longer just a normal full time bioscience undergraduate student living away from home at university.

I had been offered a job in my chosen field by a reputable American company. I was going to work in a professional, industrial, microbiology laboratory. My employment was going to be based at the plant that was within walking distance of my bed, being situated a little way up the road from my family home in Ilfracombe. With the offer of flexibility by my new boss I had made the decision to continue my studies in applied microbiology at the University of the West of England, aka UWE, situated in the city of my birth and childhood Bristol, on a part-time basis, whilst also embarking on a journey into the strange new world of full time professional employment. To be able to undertake this double life I would end up having to attend university one day a week over the next three academic years; this was due to the combination of modules I was required to pass to be able to graduate with a Bachelor of Science honours degree.

Anyone who knows me even by just a small margin will explain that I can be a little car crazy. I enjoy driving; I also enjoy weekends spent fiddling round underneath bonnets, mainly making the mistake of removing something I later find difficult to refit or am unable to remove without the purchase of a specific tool. With that fact in mind it should come as no surprise that I actually was, in a demented way, looking forward to driving the 200+ mile round trip from my home in Ilfracombe, north Devon, to the north of Bristol and back on a weekly basis. I was looking forward to it with such enthusiasm that I got a little carried away with myself. So much so that upon confirmation of my new wages, all of my meagre savings plus a small but still sizable loan were withdrawn and spent on a sports car.

The car in question was a little less than three year old purple/blue Mazda RX-8 and it was stunning. Having test driven a number of different sports coupes I knew exactly what I really wanted in a GT car, the Mazda ticked all those boxes. To this day I will defend the RX-8 as being truly brilliant, fast, comfortable, well equipped, good looking, with all the fun of having great rear wheel drive power; its controllable cornering and handling made driving it a genuinely awesome experience for someone of my mind set. Unfortunately my passion was very quickly brought crashing back down to reality. During my first trip to Bristol in the new motor it became very quickly apparent exactly how woefully bad the fuel economy of the RX-8's 1.3 litre Wankel rotary engine was. I had prepared for heavier fuel bills than my strangely efficient little 1.8 Volvo hatchback - it's an occupational hazard of sports car ownership - but reality was far more shocking that I had ever expected. However among my friends and family I am known for my eternal optimism, so the minor aggravation of having to spend a few more minutes of my time in the queue at a petrol station was soon far outweighed by the joy of the drive when finally out on an open road.

This now neatly brings me on to the second obstacle of the commute: finding an open road. The northern part of the county of Devon is blessed with a fair number of good fun roads to drive a well-balanced sports car on. Low population density, plus a terrain littered with hills and valleys make for some brilliant opportunities to test what a car is truly made of. Blasting up steep sections, feeling the back end step out when you enter a corner on the limit of the grip. Quite why country road driving is one of the reasons drop top rear wheel drive cars like the RX-8's little brother the MX-5 or BMW's Z series are so popular in this country; it sure isn't because the UK has the weather to require a convertible. The Devon countryside however is not perfect; it has a number of major flaws in terms of it being a driver's playground. As if in some sort of sadistic taunting twist of fate, as soon as you turn the key to your beautifully cleaned, exciting little sports car and open the sunroof to the warm late summer air, the roads of Devon begin to change. They morph in to a torturous hell, infested with the mobile evil that is the caravan or the horse box. Caravans, I am convinced, must either be the product of the devil, or the keepers of some form of intergalactic equilibrium, which states that the average speed of all the particles in the universe added together must remain the same at all times. You never find a caravan speeding along a country road. A caravan doing more than a crawling pace will never be, oh no, that would without doubt upset the cosmic speed limit and my guess would cause the spontaneous mid-air generation of the Higgs boson (for any reader feeling somewhat confused by the particle physics reference being made by my last statement; the Higgs boson aka the 'god particle' is the missing piece of an Einstein equation, it has only ever been theorised and simulated; never observed in nature. The large Hadron Collider; a particle accelerator near Cern in the France-Switzerland border was created to try and generate this particle in a controlled laboratory environment by smashing other sub atomic particles together. (The only problem with that idea is that the equation didn't rule out the possibility that the creation of the Higgs boson may in fact bring about the total collapse of the universe as we know it). Nature however, is not content simply with an army of caravans and their equine counterparts enforcing the laws of physics by clogging up the roads, the sports car driver has to the battle with two other consequences of rural life; tractors and runaway livestock. As far as I understand it, in a bid to avoid mounting road rage and keep traffic flowing swiftly, tractors and other cumbersome, slow moving road users are required by the Highway Code to pull over and let traffic pass on at least every third opportunity, if the tail back is three or more vehicles long. This, however, I have never witnessed. More like once they know they have three cars behind them tractors will do their level best to avoid giving any opportunity to overtake. Escaped livestock pose a completely different problem. Sheep and other livestock have been selectively bred by human beings for thousands of years. This selected evolution has been driven by a desire for more edible meat, or milk or a better quality of wool, or hide. It could be argued that this level of human intervention has also had the effect of degenerative evolution on the animal's basic survival skills. In the wild, the modern agricultural sheep would no longer be a competitive species able to survive without aid of human management. Wild four legged animals such as the deer react with a logical self-preservation pattern of behaviour when presented with a large fast moving vehicle, after the 'deer in headlights' momentary shock, they bolt for the closest hedge. Sheep however have become so accustomed to the presence of humans and their machinery being a normally positive experience that their natural instincts have been attenuated. Thanks to this; when sheep are placed in the same situation as our hypothetical deer, they often simply freeze on the spot. Some sheep have indeed managed to retain a certain amount of their ancestral 'fight or flight' response, this however often gets misinterpreted by the beast. For example; I have in the past driven round a hedge lined corner on the edge of Exmoor, to find a group of sheep standing in the middle of the road, drinking from a puddle. At this point most of the group just looked on blankly as I began breaking. One of their number decided however that the correct response to the nearly two tonnes of oncoming Volvo was in fact to run head first towards said vehicle. Luckily by the power of ABS, disc brakes and evasive manoeuvring complemented with large amounts of horn usage, collision was averted and neither the car nor the retarded lamb chop sustained any damaged during this event. I feel I may have digressed somewhat from my original point. That is to say that; driving though Devon is an experience I believe everyone should attempt at least once in their life. At times it is arguably more physically and mentally taxing than driving through a city, but also a far more rewarding journey.

Country road driving was not the only testing ground on my commute to Bristol. North Devon is both blessed and cursed by a near complete lack of motorway; the M5 skirts its way around the edge of the county. With a relatively small population thinly spread across the region, and what I can only guess is quite a limited budget, north Devon was never really going to be very high on the hit list for the motorway network. Instead what we got left with was either endless miles of indirect B roads snaking confusing across Exmoor or once you leave the motorway at M5 junction 27 you must prepare yourself for the annoyance that is the A361 'north Devon link road' – 36 miles of monotonous single track road cutting a straight line across the county. The north Devon link road in my opinion can only be described as a good idea badly executed. Being the most direct route, this road has to be used by every resident and visitor to a north Devon destination. The volume of heavy goods vehicles, caravans, and tractors make travel on this road at any real pace near impossible, to this end it is the only 36-mile long stretch of British A road I know of which can regularly take about an hour to travel the length of, even though it conforms to the national speed limit. Proponents of the link road will counter my previous description stating that the link road has a number of overtaking lanes, situated on the inclines of the hills where slow moving traffic can be passed. In response to such a valid point, I would like to ask that given the volume and variety of vehicles using it, why wasn't the whole of the bloody road not laid as a dual carriageway in the first place? Countless times I have been stuck in a queue of traffic behind some tractor or lorry, got to a hill ready to overtake only to find that the car three or so in front wants to overtake but doesn't have the power to do so on a gradient. This leaves me and all the other cars in the queue behind this individual either stuck behind the tractor for yet another eight miles or swerving wildly to cut back in on our side of the road at the very limit of the overtaking lane. As I said previously, good idea badly executed.

Lastly my commute was topped off with the monotony of the M5, M4 and M32 motorways. I have nothing really to say on motorways. They are functional, boring necessities, as any good math teacher will tell you, the quickest route from point A to point B is a straight line directly linking the two which is exactly the theory behind the motorway network. According to a friend of mine the motorway does serve a secondary function; as an illegal proving ground of the absolute maximum speed of a given vehicle, best used at around three in the morning when other traffic is non-existent, often for many miles at a time. Apparently the United Kingdom has one of the safest motorway networks in the world, I can only comment on that by saying, I have been, when I was much younger, involved in a minor motorway accident and driven away, so as far as I'm concerned we must be doing something right.

Over the following years two concepts became very apparent to me. The first was that my love of driving became quite a drain on my bank balance with the rising price of petrol. The second was that north Bristol is a complete nightmare to get in or out of at certain times of the day. Countless times have I been stuck on the M5 between junctions 18 and 17, on one occasion for more than three hours completely motionless! This occasionally put the doubt in my mind that I had made the correct decisions over job and car. These doubts were compounded by two concepts. The first being that with a low mileage car of the RX-8's calibre there are not many short and simple maintenance jobs to take up a few minutes on a Sunday morning. The other issue was Rosie's dislike of my car mainly due to its expense and non-environmentally friendly image. All these issues combined forced me to formulate a plan. This plan saw the re-kindling of my first driving passion, with the help of my family I saved all I could and soon I had the funds to once again purchase a classic Mini. Being of simple 'barn door engineering' the Mini would facilitate the answer to all my quandaries. Its body work was solid but it had several mechanical and electrical issues that I hopefully would be able to at least have an attempt at sorting out myself. Being cute, easy, and fun to drive as well as a real classic cult motor, I hoped it would also interest Rosie more than the RX-8, giving her access when she required to her own means of private transport and so could be something we could share. The idea of us sharing the Mini also meant that should I have ever not wanted to, I wouldn't have to do all the driving when we ventured out on day trips or holidays. Sharing this obligation was a concept Rosie was only vaguely interested in. So, armed with both the cute iconic classic to run to the shops in, or lend to the girlfriend, and the exciting grand touring sports car for interesting drives, I felt my life was OK and things were looking pretty good for a while.

Introduction

As a word of warning to you, my potential reader, in writing this book I have not set out simply to point out what I feel are the failures and successes with public transport. Should I have wished to do so I would have modestly written a letter of complaint for the appropriate governing body or company to then ignore as often seems to be the practice in this world. I do not intend to rant on endlessly about late trains/buses, jammed roads, lack of leg room or seating and ticket pricing. Although it's quite safe to say, these topics will inevitably be mentioned in the context of my story. I feel several thousand words slandering poor performance on such topics would be not only dreadfully boring, depressing, unreadable and therefore un-publishable, but also somewhat pointless due to it only being of interest to and therefore only read by like-minded bitter individuals. On the other hand I wish for my work to have the balance and positivity to be able to be enjoyed by anyone regardless of your personal opinion and preferences on the use of private versus public transport.

There you have it, barely a few lines in, and with the brutal power of frank honesty I have successfully destroyed any sadistic hopes of reading a completely damning report filled only with anger, hatred, and narcissism!

You may be sitting there asking yourself, what can you expect from rest of this book, and for that matter, what reason can I give to validate the time and energy you will have to expend to read it? As was pointed out to me by my girlfriend of the time, Rosie, the main female character for whom the record of these stories was initially intended. With the exception of academic technical text books and reference articles, books read for pleasure have to have both a point to be explained and a plot running through them to be worth reading. Well, as the protagonist of this collection of memorable events I wish to inform you of love in its many forms, the love between a boy and a girl, the love between man and machine, and most of all the love of life and all the splendour, as well as frustrations, of the modern world in which we live. How I believe, with the right mind set and transportation, even the daily commute can become a wondrous adventure. Through these pages I will describe to you a year in my life and I hope you enjoy reading about it. It was a magical year, which you will hopefully see as proof that when it comes to transport, both public and/or private, the perceived fact is very much stranger than fiction. At this point I would like to stress that all the events which unfold throughout this book are, to the best of my ability, recounts of my perceptions of actual events and experiences I have witnessed. This can be best described by directly quoting my mother, Pamela Jayne Elwell.

"Through the power of keen observation it seems that you, my son, have been gifted the ability to find the hidden adventure in the norm, the often overlooked beauty in the detail of everyday life."

Through these pages I hope that you begin to see, as I have, the individual Jekyll and Hyde nature of all forms of travel within the British Isles and beyond; their brilliant highs and equally epic crashing lows. All this seen from the view point of a sometimes bored and I expect somewhat slightly crazy microbiology graduate.

Finally I must apologise to anyone and everyone that I have encountered on the trains, the train station platform and in fact the bus stop and even the petrol station or road. I, with optimism, hope that if you do in fact read about yourself in this text, you are not too offended by my assessment. You have inevitably served as lab rats in what has in part ended up as a pseudo-scientific cross examination of the culture that surrounds transport, whether that be public or private in nature and how our modern society chooses which type to use and when.

Chapter One
September 2010

The final straw to my two car lifestyle came in the September of the final year of my part time degree. Due to timetabling issues, my one day per week had to change to two half days. This was in fact a logistical nightmare for me. The terms of my contract at work stated I was allowed one day per week to attend an education of benefit to my continued professional development aka CPD and position within the company; to be able to reconcile these two constraints required me to work an eight hour evening shift instead of my normal day shift, one day each week. On the face of it this would not seem so bad, unfortunately this evening shift was after three hours of lectures and at least two hours of transportation between the two locations. This also inevitably caused a greater strain on my finances by doubling the mileage I was expecting my little cars to cope with. This was the point at which I almost had to admit defeat. The Mazda simply was no longer an economically viable means of commuting the distance with such regularity without the costs impacting on other aspects of my lifestyle. Most sensible people faced with this situation would have either used the Mini much more instead or, simply sold the RX-8 and bought a small diesel hatchback.

These were categorically not options I was prepared to entertain. Some people will think my reasoning is insane but, I simply refuse to let someone else dictate what car I should be driving by their greed. I will remain behind the wheel of a fun, sporty vehicle until ownership of such a car is truly beyond the realms of possibility for me to do so. In deciding that my love of driving the car of my choice far outstripped my requirement for actual transportation, I had to look at the alternatives.

This is the point of inception, the true beginning of this text. Travelling by train for a least half of my weekly journeys brought the costs within my budget, while still allowing both the RX-8 and Mini to remain mine and part or my flamboyant lifestyle. It is at this point that I will reintroduce Rosie and give her a proper introduction, as she became a considerable factor in the decision to subject myself to public transport on a regular basis. You see, Rosie, being the wonderfully geeky, socially troubled and highly opinionated person she was, had after a troubled year initially studying a bachelor of arts in international development at the University of East Anglia in Norwich, decided to reapply to study a degree in mathematics at the University of Exeter. Being that by this point in time she was a second year student, she rented a room in a house in Exeter, a few streets away from Polsloe Bridge, one of the city's inner suburban train stations. This gave me a great opportunity to be able to spend the night at Rosie's and catch the train from Exeter to Bristol at a semi sensible time in the morning instead of the alternative of driving from my home to the closest national west coast mainline train station, Tiverton Parkway, just to pick up the same train. The Tiverton option would also see me having to wake at five a.m. to make the journey. As if I had somehow once again become a teenager without a driving licence I became used to the pros and cons of travel on public transport.

Chapter Two
Lost property

Lost property and public transport have forever had a troubled relationship; the chance of an item being misplaced or left behind somewhere is inevitably high when the system is run to such a tight schedule. In recent times, public address system announcements everywhere remind you to keep guard looking for unattended packages. This nanny state of paranoia has been escalating over the years due to a combination of health and safety regulation, acts of terrorism, and antisocial behaviour the world over. Now, I do not want to upset any poor soul who has lost a loved one due an act of terrorism or any of the world conflicts that have arisen seeking retribution for such acts. I agree that security needs to be high in important buildings or high risk areas. Bristol or Tiverton Parkway stations however I do not really see as high profile targets. In Bristol Parkway's case mainly because it's a good five-minute walk away from any other large highly populated building. As for Tiverton, this is ten minutes' walk from any other sign of life. Yet every few minutes there are public safety announcements telling you that you need to be wary of suitcases, and mistrusting of your fellow passengers. This is supported by a number of posters displaying who is to be contacted in an emergency and how this can be done. To me it all seems a bit much, and arguably anti-social in itself, but then who am I other than just another face in the crowd trying to find my train? Forgetting for a moment all about national security and public safety issues, I would prefer to take a short time to discuss problems that can occur when even a purely harmless item of luggage is lost on public transport. In keeping with the general theme of this book I will be drawing on a couple of colourful examples that I know of to help illustrate my point. Being fortunate enough to have never left something on the train myself I have however been witness to several others not being so fortunate. The first of these events takes us to I believe the first week in October of the year in question. It was 7:20 a.m. on Tuesday morning and I was queuing on platform five of Exeter St David's. As the train I was waiting for arrived it was clearly marked as being the cross country service from Plymouth bound for Edinburgh. As the train drew to a stop a short young looking man could be seen looking rather flustered and wrestling with his baggage in his seat. By my estimation he was in his mid to late teenage years and seemed to have a seat free next to him. Moments later I boarded the train and prepared myself to walk down the train's narrow corridor, as I did so someone a little shorter than me and nowhere near as bulky as my frame darted awkwardly past me as I momentarily stood and looked out of the little porthole window in the adjacent door. The doors quickly slammed shut behind me. Turning to look down the length of the carriage I could not see the young man that I had spied from the platform and assumed he must have left the train in the great crowd of people that had walked past me on the platform. Knowing the train was going to get progressively busier the closer we came to Bristol, I decided to find the first empty seat close the toilet, which was where I would sit. This turned out to be the seats just inside the carriage's internal door on what was, at this station, the platform side of the train. Even though it was the standard class the carriage looked comfortable. Disaster struck as I sat down. It was purely my own fault for not checking the seat swab before planting my weight on it but as I sat down I noticed quickly the discomfort of a small hard rectangular object unfortunately placed between me and the seat's swab. Triggering a few moments of me awkward shuffling round. This culminated in the offensive object being removed and falling gently on the carpeted floor between my feet. Having now settled down and got myself comfortable in the seat I ignored the confused gazes of the other passengers, removed my hoody and attempted to inspect the cause of my previous discomfort. This turned out to be a mobile phone. To be more exact it was, on closer inspection, a new model of touch screen Nokia similar to but down the range of my own device for mobile communication. Having the knowledge of the object's worth, both in terms of financial value and social value, I was trapped for a few minutes with the dilemma of whether or not to remove the sim card and in an underhanded manner sell the object online, as the old saying goes, 'finders, keepers loser's weepers'. On the other hand I thought I should take the moral high ground and do a good deed trying to return the device to its proper owner, thinking that not trying to return it was an immoral idea that may also end up backfiring on me, breaking my own run of good luck not losing things on public transport. I settled on the idea that I would do my level best to get the object back to its rightful home. Unfortunately that then left me with another problem to think over. How to actually get it there and for that matter how to find out where 'there' was in the first place? My first option was to wait till the ticket collector came around and hand it to him, letting the official channels deal with the problem. At first this seemed an obvious and easy way out. My other options involved more effort on my part but allowed me to feel more instrumental in the completion of the good deed. I settled on trying to contact the phone's owner. In making this choice, I had once again left myself in a quandary. I didn't really feel like making a phone call to someone I didn't know in case it all went wrong and they ended up convinced I was a thief of some kind. On the other hand I didn't want to read the person's text messages to find someone to contact in case I saw something I shouldn't. By the time my train pulled away from Taunton I finally gathered up the courage to sort the situation and summoned the strength and clear head to try looking through the phone's address book for a number relating to home or family. After a few moments of scrolling I did indeed find a number marked 'home' that I could ring. A woman picked up the other end of the line. After explaining the situation so far as I understood the woman filled me in with some details.

The phone belonged to her son. From the description she gave I came to the conclusion that he must have been both the young man I had seen from the platform as the train approached earlier and probably was also the short person who had run past me after almost missing his stop. He was an A' level student at college in Exeter. He lived near Plymouth. I do not wish to offend anybody here but having been there several times I have come to the opinion that Plymouth is not my most favourite of places and is generally somewhere I avoid going unless it is absolutely necessary. Nevertheless I agreed to retain the phone until I had packaged it up and could send it by recorded delivery back to its unfortunate owner. The situation was not so easily rectified. As the train pulled out of Bristol Temple Meads, Bristol's central train station, and the penultimate stop on my journey, the problematic phone began to ring. I answered it and was about to inform the caller of the situation when it transpired to be the phone's owner phoning to make his own arrangements to retrieve the device. He requested to know where I was going to be getting off the train. He then made it clear that I was to hand the item in at the station manager's office with the instructions that it was to be collected later that day by him. A request I filled with great haste and urgency upon my eventual arrival at Bristol Parkway.

Chapter Three
Life, Death and Lectures

On my way between Exeter and Bristol I came close on one occasion to witnessing some poor soul's death; on the other hand I also had on two occasions the strange good fortune of helping out, in some small manner, on the day a new soul was brought into the world. I shall start by getting the more morbid memories out of the way, hopefully allowing me to end this chapter on a more positive note. It just so happened that two of these events occurred within hours of each other, on the day I will forevermore refer to as the day of life, death, and lectures!

It was a cold late autumn morning at Exeter St David's. My train was already running a couple of minutes late when it finally drew in at platform five. This was of no major concern to me, for as long as it did not become any more behind schedule the only difference it would make to my day would be the need to jog instead of walk from Bristol Parkway to my university campus in order to make it to my lecture on time. As I got seated on the train I noted that it was unusually quiet. This I hoped would somehow help the train make up for its shortfall in time keeping. Without me really paying much attention ten minutes passed by without the train making a move. It was only once I had finished the green apple and then the bottle of orange squash which Rosie has very lovingly supplied me with which were meant for my lunch that I did finally notice the train's delay was increasing. A feeling and sensation of mild panic beginning to play on my mind, I started to deal with the concept that I would at this rate turn up late for the first section of my lecture, something I avoid doing at all costs.

It was at that bizarre moment the relatively tranquil silence of the near empty cabin was broken by an address from the train manager explaining the situation at hand. It was explained that the train was locked up and ready to depart from the station but could not be granted clearance to do so due to officers of the British Transport Police having difficulty wrestling with an individual who was insisting on messing around on the tracks just north of the station. I should also make it clear at this point that although I try my best to be respectful to those who are, I am definitely not religious. This doesn't mean however that I don't have faith; it's just that my faith is humanist and comes from the idea that scientific endeavour will eventually explain all the mysteries of this world and social acceptance, cooperation, and equality are the future we should all strive to towards. I also believe life should be preserved wherever possible and it takes a lot for someone to upset me to the point that I would wish for an unfortunate event to fall upon them. With that in mind please picture me sitting there on my train, panicked by the fact I was running late and now overcome with a feeling of sorrow for this individual and the situation as a whole. I was helplessly just sitting there hoping this clearly troubled individual would see sense and let the police take them away, hoping the British Transport Police would see to it that they got any help that they clearly required, and finally hoping that this was to be the worst point of my day. A few more minutes passed and the train began to move off. As it did so I found myself unable to look out of the window worried by the mental image of what I may have to see, such as bloody body parts scattered by the track side. As the train picked up speed the manager made another announcement. This time with a far more upbeat and pleasant tone. All was in fact well and there was even the possibility of making up some of the delay.

As it turned out we arrived at Bristol Parkway only some five minutes late. I however still missed the first hour of my three hour lecture. Only this time for a generally more pleasant reason than the one previously discussed. This was due to me choosing to do a good deed as I do as often as possible.

Leaving the station and taking two left turns to walk behind the insurance brokers and through the edge of Harry Stoke I could see a man pacing small circles on the pavement near to a mini roundabout that I often passed by. He was attempting unsuccessfully to stop and engage in conversation with every person who walked by. Four individuals consecutively ignored him which perplexed me as his body language did not seem threatening. Indeed he was an average man, average in terms of looks body shape, dress sense and I would guess around his late thirties. I crossed the road so that I could be the next to intersect him and find the cause of his troubled nature.

The day, it turned out, was to be the joyous occasion when the man in question was to become a father. The birth of a child is often a stressful day for all concerned, but most of all the stress is normally focused around the woman in labour and happens within the walls of a hospital. The situation was such that our somewhat stressed father to be was meant to be making his way to Southmead Hospital to be with his wife who had begun her contractions. It has to be said that Southmead is quite a common hospital in the Bristol area for the birth process; I was delivered there in the mid-afternoon of the 23rd of February 1986. Our expectant father came from a small town just outside of Bristol; upon hearing that his partner had been taken in to hospital; he had jumped in his car and sped off in search of the hospital. Having gotten a little lost he ended up running out of petrol near Parkway Station scarcely more than a few miles from his intended destination. This was compounded by a lack of money and phone credit - he was effectively stranded. His saving grace came in the knowledge that his in-laws were on their way to meet him and his partner at the hospital and so there was the potential that they could be contacted and asked to pick him up on the way. Unfortunately all he knew was that they would be coming towards Bristol from the west along the eastbound M4 motorway but he was himself lost and unsure as to where they would be able to meet him or how to get to his current location. This is the part I played that morning; if I had any money on me that day I was prepared to have given it to him, as he kept showing me photos of his family and his identification to try and prove to me his plight. Unfortunately I had a habit of paying for everything on debit card and often I used to walk around with very little in the way of cash on my person. For that reason, all I could do was lend him a shoulder to cry on and then when more composed help him get a bearing for where he was and then help him to both contact and explain directions to his position to his in-laws as they approached Bristol from the west. Once we were both satisfied that I had done all I could to assist this gentleman and his family I made haste and sprinted the remainder of the distance to my lecture as fast as I could, arriving exactly in time for the first tea break which gave my perfect opportunity to apologise and explain to my lecturer the reasoning for my absence during the first hour, thankfully my lecturer that day, Shona Nelson, took my words on board and agreed that my course of action was honourable and a valid justification for my lateness. It was also a stroke of luck that the topics covered during the section I had missed were a subject area that, thanks to my employment, I already had a strong working knowledge of, allowing me to seamlessly integrate myself in to the class as the lecture continued. Thankfully my journey back to Barnstaple that afternoon was not so dramatic with the only break from the monotony of a boring train journey being when I found a discarded national lottery scratch card on the floor which turned out to be an unclaimed small prize of five pounds, which I later used to buy a number of grocery items to bolster Rosie's food cupboard and treat her a little as a display of my affection and desire for her well-being.

Chapter Four
Sandwiches

I must apologise for what is to follow. I do not wish to bitch and curse but I'm afraid on this subject I have to, I'm also pretty sure that this will get me in to hot water, with someone, somewhere, but sod it, I need to get this off my chest. Train station food outlets, almost all of them, can kiss my ass!

A lot of people reading this I have no doubt will have had dealings with these facilities. Some of you may even work in them, if this is the case then allow me to quote the comedian Al Murray's pub landlord character;

"Don't get upset, this is not directed at you, it's a generalisation, which means it possibly includes you."

From my experiences with purchasing food from a number of these establishments I have the opinion that the majority are all run (at a corporate level) by money grabbing sadists, who have no clue what the world of the average public transport user is like. I feel genuinely sorry for all the staff that has to work for these franchises. I feel sorry for them because they have must have to put up with so much every single day often for minimal pay.

First off the food is basically mass produced rubbish, thrown together and then reheated by either some poor sap with little or no qualifications, or a student who can't actually see straight due the quantity of vodka still pumping its way around their blood stream. I understand that this a business and that the companies supplying these outlets wish to make as big a profit as possible so pre-producing the basic components of their menus and simplifying customer options cuts costs and preparation time, but this idea has been taken to the extreme. From what I can recall with only a small number of exceptions I haven't once actually enjoyed anything I have eaten at a station.

Talking of costs, with the fact that almost all the menu is produced in bulk, on the cheap, how is it at all fair to charge the astronomical prices that you will find on platforms up and down the country? I object just as much to the price of the third party items as the goods actually produced by the franchise. For example, I am perfectly happy to pay, say £3 for a somewhat badly produced cheese sandwich, simply because I can see the face of the poor guy who's had to spend the last eight hours of his life assembling 500 of them before he can clock off, make his way home to his family, and cry himself to sleep. I object however to the idea that I then have to pay nearly two pounds for a bottle of popular branded cola that I know could be bought for a quarter of the price at a supermarket (and yet even then the supermarket still make a profit on it).

Another common failure of these franchises is in customer service. As a potential sale, yes I would like to see someone who is happy, smiling and enthusiastic about their job. There is no denying the over the top American concept that pleasant staff makes sales easier. On the other hand, it would be more beneficial to me to be able to actually speak to someone who knew how to answer questions about the products, instead of just regurgitating pre-programmed information less a torrent of verbal excrement topped off with a completely faked smile.

In my mind, this approach to service is a bit like a bowl of fake fruit to a desert island castaway. On the face of it, it's perfectly fine, but once you begin to analyse what you have been presented with, it becomes annoyingly lacking in substance, and therefore loses any point of it being there at all. I'm not saying that presentation is not important. What I I'm saying that, a little less money spent on the pointless bollocks, like making sure that all the staff must give out receipts even when it isn't really necessary to do so, would allow a little more time informing the staff how to respond to questions such as, what the hell is the different between a 'flat white' and a latté? A real query I overheard one day while queuing, and which was answered with, "I'm not sure, it's new, I think it has something to do with the milk."

This has now led me to an opportunity to explain a little game that I like to play when having to purchase something at a train station. I'm not sure if this is a national requirement but I can say for certain that all the station outlets I have been to subscribe to a policy that any purchase has to be supplied with a receipt. Stuck to the side of the tills, you will find a tiny little unobtrusive blue and green sign; this sign is basically worded as follows:

"If you are not given a receipt with your change then your purchase is free of charge, as long as you inform the member of staff of their error directly."

I only noticed this by chance one day while waiting for a member of staff to actually materialise. I have to admit at this point that when paying with currency in note form or on debit card then I have never failed to be supplied with said receipt. Reading this sign got me thinking and in my boredom I began to get pleasure from a simple game, one so simple and potentially money saving that I urge you to partake if given the opportunity. The game is to pay with the exact money required, to the penny and completely in loose change. This often completely bamboozles the vast majority of these shop workers I have tested it on. The reactions do range widely. From closing the till and walking off (which for me is the best possible outcome as I then get the pleasure of pointing out what they have done and so claiming my money back therefore making it a free lunch) to the unfortunate consequence of wasting paper by handing me a completely pointless, unnecessary receipt without asking if I actually wanted/required it. The reaction which gives me the most humour for my money however, is timing how long the person on the other side of the counter takes thinking over the dilemma. It's brilliant fun; you can almost see cogs turning as the thought process happens deep in their minds. If life was a comic book they would have a thought bubble above their head saying something along the lines of:

"Give them the change and remember to give them the receipt, give them the change and receipt, hang on there is no change. Help what do I do? Mummy I'm confused, this wasn't covered on the training day!"

Some people may call me twisted but I really do get a sadistic kick out of watching this happen. I look at it as pay back for the rubbish standard of service and/or product that I have had to put up with.

Chapter Five
Platforms

The train station platform opens an interesting opportunity for people watching and the study of the more colourful individuals that public transport subjects us all to. One such individual is the trainspotter.

I have to tread very carefully around the hobby of trainspotting, and the people who pursue it because my late father, a man that I had a great deal of respect for, has in the past been one of these nutters himself. Trainspotting, like all hobbies, creates its own internal segregation in to sub-populations that vary in their fanaticism for their subject. Within any randomly selected group of trainspotters there will be people such as my father, keen amateur or semi-professional photographers with an interest or background in engineering. As with most hobbies these are the people who make up the majority of the ranks of its followers, the mild cases so to speak.

I have to say I can easily understand the appeal, the idea of an afternoon out sat in the summer sun with a picnic waiting for the slow motion passage of some maintained piece of locomotive history, so that you can get a few snaps which you then sell to a magazine for a couple of pounds. The idea actually seems quite an amiable one, although I am unsure if this is actually my own novel opinion or an example of Pavlovian 'classical conditioning' thanks to my father. Returning to my original point, this is the outlook of the majority of trainspotters; train spotting, however, has been shown to have examples of much more fanatical individuals within its ranks.

I encountered one such loony on my arrival at platform two of Bristol Parkway one afternoon. While walking down the stairs to the platform I noticed the area directly at the bottom of the stairs was unusually clear for the time of day. Moments later I was presented with the reason for the apparent lack of people. Standing at the bottom of the stairs was a young man, mid-twenties in age. Now I must interject with an admission, I cannot conclusively proclaim that this person was in fact a trainspotter, but I can say with a strong degree of certainty that should he in fact not have been a trainspotter, he may have been mentally ill. I have to also admit at this point to a small habit of my own. When assessing someone on the grounds of first visual impressions, I pay only a little attention to their clothes. Their shoes on the other hand I find to be somewhat telling of aspects of someone's personality.

Using this potential trainspotter as an example of my point, I always become unnerved by adult males who wear cheap, black, Velcro fastening trainers. These I am convinced, are a tell-tale sign of some sort of mental affliction or a complete lack of style and self-image. When these are accompanied by trousers too short in the leg to meet said shoes, white sports socks and thick rimmed tortoise shell glasses, this combination of bad dress sense should have really set my alarm bells ringing. On this occasion it was somehow overlooked by my powers of self-preservation. For the ten minutes that we had to share space on a platform, myself and the other passengers of the following trains were at the mercy of this complete fruit cake. The nutter in question devoted himself to near continually reading aloud, the digital message board which displayed the information regarding the next few trains. As well as reciting already common knowledge, he could be heard attempting to mimic the tune played before the audible announcements. In between repeating this torrent of information, he managed to maintain a conversation with himself over what was meant by the term HST (high speed train) and that he suspected the next train would in fact be a HST, due the route it was running from Edinburgh to Plymouth. This display was, for all who observed it, more than slightly uncomfortable. As my train approached the platform a worrying scenario formed within my head. This thought was terrifying and caused me to furtively inspect the rest of the platform for the number of people standing on it. The idea in question was that the train was going to be busy, and therefore the probability of having to spend a further hour in close proximity to the train obsessed nutter would be greatly increased. Moments later I was my relief presented with additional evidence that he was in fact a trainspotter. Everyone on the platform rushed for a carriage door while he just stood there looking at the train's name plate smiling away to himself as he did so; not attempting to actually get on board.

Train-spotting psychos aside, platforms host a bewildering demographic range of people. While sitting at any station waiting for a train, one of the little things that makes public transport worth writing about is the interactions between oneself and other service users. This can take many forms, from conservation to simply pass the time to quite contemplative people watching and social commentary.

On the subject of conversation, top of the bill on random conversations I must recount begin with the simple and ordinary question, 'what time is it?' The person in question was a man whose name was never volunteered, so for the purpose of informality and familiarity I will henceforth refer to him as John. Our time together on platform three of Exeter's mainline station (St David's) was the 50 minute wait between the arrival of the Plymouth bound train we had coincidentally both stepped off, and the arrival of the Barnstaple bound train I was about to step on. John was a tall man in his mid-40s, who had a very obvious interest in hiking and as it transpired, ornithology. At this point I have to explain that I enjoy walking through forests and camping holidays with my partner and/or friends; I even enjoy completely back to nature wilderness survival weekends with only a knife, a saw, cup and a mirror as available equipment, but hiking in a regimented militaristic manner just for the sake of covering ground, I have never really seen much point in (this was one of the few points of disagreement between Rosie and myself. Rosie had long been a member of the air training corps, and spends several weekends a year just walking from point to point with no real goal other than to get there first and prove the fact that it can be done often without any real competitive element, something she became very good at). Neither have I found the idea of bird watching a captivating pastime. It holds a similar opinion in my mind as trainspotting, only a shade more difficult from the point of the unpredictable nature of the subject matter. However I also see it as having more of a purpose, as you are observing a biological entity for which there is no identical replacement, not a machine where a carbon copy could be produced if required. It was blindingly apparent from his attire that John would have had a few things more in common with my good lady than myself. Starting as I always do with the shoes, these were brown, utilitarian steel toe caps that were well worn, but showed signs of meticulous upkeep. This footwear was complimented with army surplus acquired camouflage print trousers, a blue fleece jumper, and heavy green jacket. Before we had even spoken, a 'pigeon hole' (pardon the rather awful pun) on John's interests had been firmly cemented in my mind by the fact that he was carrying binoculars, a 55 litre backpack, and strangely, a snake skin effect cowboy hat.

As previously described the conversation between me and John was initiated by him asking the time. Anyone who has ever spent any time at all in a train station will understand how daft a scenario this seemingly normal event actually was. On average (I have worked this out statistically, trust me) the time between some audible announcements at a mainline train station is approximately two minutes. So with all joking aside when John asked the time I have to admit to being somewhat suspicious of his nature. For a split second, I was lost in a world of uncertainty; was this man mentally ill and suffering from such severe short-term memory loss that he was unable to recall what he must have heard only two minutes ago over the station's public address system? Was he mentally deficient in his understanding of how to operate a watch? Or was this some sort of ploy to gently engage me in conversation? It was then that I realised more than just a spilt second had passed since the question had been asked, and that John had probably by now begun to wonder if he had in fact found someone mentally deficient in their ability to respond to a simple question. The tension was relieved by my reply that it was in fact seven minutes past three. I said this while pointing in the direction of a digital message board, which hung from the roof only a few feet away from our seating. Thus adding to the irony of the original question being asked. After a few moments of awkward silence John opened communications again. This time proclaiming the statement that he thought the weather was less than desirable. A comment that I had no choice but to agree with as it was in fact raining so hard that I had myself began to wonder if trains could get waterlogged. The next thought that ran through my mind in hindsight may have been acted on in haste. The dilemma that I was faced with was simple - do I continue letting this person engage me in what was basically turning in to a one sided conversation, or did I venture something of my own? Not wanting to seem rude I opted for the idea of starting a topical conversation. After a few moments of silence in which I hopelessly searched for a relevant talking point I blindly over looked the possibility of enquiring about his hobbies and began in a minor way to panic. Then like an involuntary bodily function I opened our communication with; "What are your thoughts on the price of cheese?" as a talking point. For most sane individuals, the price of cheese would rarely enter the mind if not standing in the dairy isle of a supermarket, but this seems to be my safely blanket of conversation starters; I guarantee if you have nothing to say or nothing in common with someone you happen to have been placed next to at a formal function, the price of cheese will break the ice like little else. After the initial shock of my statement had settled, I had to explain my reasoning for it. John was receptive to this concept of shock tactic conversation initiation, commenting that it certainly did not require a minimum standard of intelligence or education with which to have a useful input to the debate and therefore was a topic that could span the cultural, class and generation divides.

Chapter Six
Kowalski Drives Again

As the title of this section suggests it is not simply focused on trains and public transport as a source of comedy cannon fodder, turning once again to discuss private transportation of the motorised variety. In writing it, I hope to have shown the somehow completely bonkers nature of transport in general, whether that be public or in fact private. Public transport is, as the name implies, a means of transportation that is openly available to the mass populous, which means no matter how well, or for that matter how poorly it is executed, the mere presence of it can only be a good thing for a nation. The only true failing with public transport is the fact that it is public and therefore has to fit the needs of the majority, so from an individual's perspective it will forever fall short of perfect. It is due to this shortfall that I must now describe the sort of situation where private transport is king: the crisis or the last minute decision.

An example whereby my little purple sports car became an invaluable asset to me was brought about by a problem I encountered during my final few months at university. As part of the final year process of a degree in science it is often required that you produce a research project. This demonstrates a multitude of skills; experiment design, good laboratory practice, time keeping, project management, analytical understanding, and the ability to convey oneself in the form of presentations and reports. Due to the part time nature of my attendance my project was performed over two years; this was not a problem for the most part, the problem came with the submission of the final report. You see, when I began the project module I was given a handbook of information which outlined the assessment format and submission dates, which I printed off and stuck to my notice board so it was in plain sight while at my computer working each day. What I was unaware of a year and a bit later when sitting reading the comments I had been given on my current rough draft was that, that year the final report submission for part time students had been updated without my knowledge; it had changed, keeping it in line with that of the current cohort of full time students. This meant that where I had planned and scheduled my time around the idea that I had over a month in which to correct my draft and get it reworked several times over as I normally would, in reality it needed to be printed off, bound and handed in only fourteen hours later. Put another way, by two o'clock the next day. In mad panic, I phoned Rosie as I hadn't ever missed a deadline and didn't want to start doing so with the single most important piece of work in the whole of my academic career thus far. Rosie to her credit gave me the best thing I could have wished for at that place and time - a service for which part of me will forever be in her debt. First she asked me to email her a copy of my draft along with any comments that had been made. She then instructed me to gather everything I needed to work together and drive to Exeter. Now, for the benefit of anyone confused by the title of this section, what you are expected to understand is that it makes reference to one of the great cult films of the late sixties/ early seventies – *Vanishing Point*. In the film, Kowalski, an ex-cop framed for something that wasn't his fault, is missioning through the night in a supercharged

American muscle car trying to get 1500 miles in fifteen hours, or to put it another way, attempt to drive around 100 miles an hour for fifteen hours straight. He is basically travelling alone and desperately trying to outrun the crooked cops responsible for the injustice that he was the fall guy for. His only true ally comes in the form of a blind radio DJ named Supersoul, with whom he has some sort of psychic connection, which was previously unknown to either of them. Ever since I first saw the film at the age of eighteen it has always come to mind whenever I find myself driving through the night, oh boy what a night that was. After putting the phone down at 11:20 a.m. I was knocking on Rosie's door in Exeter by 12.30 p.m., something that would not have been possible had the train been my only form of transport. From that moment on Rosie and I worked through the night until the early morning when I drove us to Exeter university in time to be the first people through the door of Exeter university print shop (UWE also has a print shop but they have a rule that they require delivery of works to be printed at least twenty-four hours before pick up, a time frame I didn't have). Within an hour and a half I had two copies of my 120-page report colour printed and bound and ready as they could be. Walking her to her lecture hall, I kissed Rosie goodbye promising to return to her that evening. I now had some three hours to make it to UWE and hand my work in for submission on time. Although this was a journey that would have been possible on public transport, the fact that my beautiful sports car had served me so handsomely so far that day coupled with the fact that if I left it there I would have to pay substantially for parking charges, I hopped in the Mazda and cruised due north through the countryside till I caught up with the M5 motorway where I once again burned rubber Kowalski style all the way to UWE.

Chapter Seven
Noises from the Quiet Carriage

On modern national train routes most trains often have quiet zones where passengers are requested to keep their noise levels down and respect the other people around them. That said, this sometimes does not work out how you may expect it to. During my final exam period I had to be in university on three consecutive mornings. Again Rosie came to my aid allowing me to use her house in Exeter as a base for that week to save me the hassle and expense of travelling from home each day as I had the week off from work. This had a number of advantages, the most obvious being that I got to spend more time in her company. This also opened up a previously unforeseen opportunity to take a later train back between Bristol and Exeter, allowing me to spend a few hours indulging in what some would call retail therapy in the centre of Bristol, the city of my childhood as well as that of at least the last three generations of my paternal bloodline. It is therefore a city that I feel a great love for. My shopping trip was a success as I would return loaded up with new couple of shirts, ties and an expensive belt not forgetting equally expensive designer underwear I would have to keep hidden from Rosie until I had destroyed my receipts. At about seven o'clock I made my way back to Temple Meads station to catch the next train heading southwest. As the train drew in to the platform the train looked very crowded, so crowded that my hopes of getting a seat fell rapidly through the floor in front of me. Taking an evening train is a completely different experience to making the same journey early in the day. At a later hour the train takes on a far more eerie atmosphere. A colleague of mine by the name of Roger has previously discussed having a similar sensation when travelling on night-time buses. On this occasion, as the train was so very busy before it got to Bristol Temple Meads and with the crushing thought that I should have booked a seat I was anticipating the reality that I would be unfortunately forced to stand. I gradually shuffled through the train. As I did so I became aware that my fellow passengers had a great reluctance in making eye contact. Not just with me but with each other, as if the feeling of unease and mistrust detailed moments ago seemed to be a unanimous concept that came from evening train travel. As I passed a young man napping on an enormous bag full of dirty shirts that he was obviously taking home from university in the hope of his parents washing, I became aware of strange noises emanating from the supposedly quiet zone which was the next carriage along. These sounds were a bizarre combination of sexual grunts, moans, and pounding acid techno, mixed with the occasional misshapen chord from a badly tuned acoustic guitar. Altogether it sounded as I guess a folk band would if they decided to rehearse their Glastonbury Festival Avalon stage set list, on the set of a porn film, being filmed at a night club in Ibiza. Or put another way, completely wrong on so many levels. That was one carriage, that even near empty, I could not bring myself to search for a seat in.

Chapter Eight

My Evenings Out on the Town in Crediton and the Central Dogma of Genetics

Once again I find myself required to delve further back in time to explain the title of this chapter and its relevance as back story to the events of this time frame. During Rosie's first year in Exeter I had the great fortune of meeting a man named Stuart Derbyshire. We met by both responding to an advert on a musicians' classifieds website. The advert had been posted by a guitar playing, singer-songwriter named Christian who was interested in jamming with other individuals of a similar nature. Christian lived in the south east corner of Exeter, and Stuart lived in the village of Crediton some twelve miles northwest of Exeter. It was a village that I often chose to drive through when visiting Exeter by car. Crediton station is also one the major stops on the train between Barnstaple and Exeter. After several messages back and forth the three of us agreed to meet. Being that I was already in Exeter for the weekend spending some time with my love and her university pals whom I got on with quite well, I first met up with Christian on the Friday night. Unfortunately Stuart couldn't attend that meeting as his message read that he was on call and so had to stay in Crediton. Christian was a good laugh and someone I liked within a short conversation. From a third person perspective it probably didn't seem like we would have much in common but as the conversation continued I felt more and more at home with him. A relaxed feeling that I knew Rosie shared as she was not showing any signs of discomfort, she often displayed quite unsettled and anxious body language around new people, a personality trait I was helping her overcome with my hyper social will-talk-to-anyone kind of nature. In the morning after a relatively quiet night having a laid back drink with Christian in one of mine and Rosie's favourite pubs in Exeter, The Old Firehouse, which it transpired was also Christian's place of employment, I woke feeling quite fresh and happy in the knowledge that I had made a friend and what's more it had been a light evening where Rosie and I had only drank two pints each. Discussing it over breakfast, I decided the following evening I would drive to Crediton and attempt to meet with Stuart for the first time having deduced from his text messages that he must have been a member of the fire service. Unfortunately due to the commitments of work my new friend Christian was unable to join me in this, as was Rosie who already had a function to attend because of being a part of a student based charity fundraising group. Luckily my friend Nick, a frustrated drummer without a kit at the time, was on hand to give me some company. That evening, my suspicions over Stuart's chosen career were partially correct. What I mean is that Stuart turned out to be an electrical engineer by trade but one who led a double life as a retained fireman - a weekend hero. Pulling up and parking somewhat awkwardly in the centre of the dark car park at Crediton's fire station Nick and I sat in the dark and waited. Some ten minutes later and seemingly from nowhere a tall and very trim man knocked on the passenger door. Opening the door and sitting next to me in the front of the car the imposing and ruggedly handsome chap introduced himself as the man we had been waiting for. Moments later we decided that under instructions from Stu I would drive up the road and park outside the Wetherspoon's pub in the centre of Crediton high street where the three of us would enjoy a couple of drinks, non-alcoholic in mine and Stuart's cases and share some food. It was clear from his outfit and shoes that Stuart's musical taste was heavily influenced by American neo- punk groups such as the Offspring. This was not a problem for either me or Nick, but I felt it could make for difficult times once Christian became involved in the mix. This was due to Christian having a much more British Indy rock 'n'& roll influenced musical style. As for Nick and I, we both bridged the gap having individual things in common with Stu, Christian and each other. After a few drinks I explained to Stu and Nick the running order of events from the previous night and was convinced that the four of us should all get to know each other better, even if no lasting band was eventually produced. The merger would undoubtedly help us all grow our individual art forms and improve as musicians. At the end of the evening I dropped Stuart back off at the fire station, at the time completely unaware that he actually lived directly opposite on the other side of the road. Eventually I returned to Rosie's university accommodation eager to hear any news of her evening, and to explain that I felt she had temporarily missed out on meeting another wonderful friend, concluding with the idea that Stu and Christian would be people whom I would like to meet up with regularly. This in my mind worked well, what with them both living in relative proximity to Rosie.

Therefore over the next few years Crediton became a regular stop on my journeys to and from Exeter by either car or train. I have enjoyed a number of evenings visiting Stu in a completely sober manner so that I could still drive on to Exeter or back home from there. In contrast to this, there have been number of evenings when Stu has not been on call and I have travelled by train to share a beverage with him. Out of all such evenings the one which will forever stick in my mind is known as the one involving the central dogma of genetics.

In several branches of science, molecular biology being a good example, you can find ideas that underpin and explain the majority of the observed phenomena that has been recorded. These ideas are not so black or white cut that they are taught as rules that have to be obeyed; this is mainly due to knowledge of special cases in nature where they are not. They are therefore given the title of dogma. When it comes to talking about genetics, the science that studies the code in which is written the instructions on how biological organisms are constructed, one such dogma is that DNA makes RNA which in turn makes proteins. It had been a Wednesday much like any other and I had caught the train down to Rosie's house. The only difference was that this evening Rosie had an important meeting to attend which I was unable to tag along to, as she was endeavouring to be voted in as treasurer for the Exeter University Expedition Society that she enjoyed being a part of. Although I understood the stress that she was opening herself up to should she get elected, I hoped the evening would go well and that she was to be successful. I supported her fully in her plight, for multiple reasons the most important being that it was something Rosie felt she really wanted to do, and over the years both of us had benefitted individually from conversations and friendships that had come from her involvement with the society. Finally I knew that the position would look good on her C.V. for years to come, irrespective of the specific career path she finally chose to pursue. For the reasons above, I was perfectly happy to entertain myself for the evening while Rosie was out. It turned out that evening that Stuart had the following day off and although he was unable to leave Crediton due to a lack of car, he was interested in having a drink with me. Getting a train back up the line as far a Crediton I spent the evening playing pool and drinking cider and discussing music with my friend until such a time that I could return to Exeter and find out how Rosie had got on. I'm not sure as to why I felt the need to, but as we sat at the station waiting for my train, I decided to explain to Stu the basics of genetics and how DNA is arranged in humans as two intertwined and complimentary helical strands of molecules called bases which together are known as the double helix. Also that within these two strands every three of these bases make up a codon, and a series of codons makes up a gene, which in most cases codes some more complex biological structures and/or functions such the components of a cell membrane. I couldn't seem to stop myself rabbiting on about how in humans DNA is copied out using a set of temporary equivalent molecules called RNA bases in a process called transcription and the resulting strands of RNA are used by a process known as translation, as instructions telling the cells of the body how to build biological constructs known as proteins. Furthermore, proteins are effectively the building blocks of the cells themselves. By the time I had finished I was sure Stu must have been wishing for the speedy arrival of my now somewhat late train to rid him of this biology lecturing half-drunk nutcase I had become. To my surprise it turned out that Stu had not only found my impromptu lecture of interest, but was excited to enquire about working examples I could explain to further emphasise my point. I began once again to talk about genetics while this time walking in small circles around the empty platform trying to keep myself warm despite the fact I was wearing a thick blue hoody. The cold wind felt like it was blowing straight through me, which was an altogether bizarre and rare occurrence as I am known to friends and family as normally being near completely impervious to temperature, usually able to comfortably wear shorts and a vest in January or a three piece suit with overcoat in the middle of summer.

Chapter Nine
The Day My Train Stopped

It was very early on a cold winter morning in Exeter; Rosie and I had shared breakfast and we had prepared ourselves for our respective days in lectures and kissed each other goodbye. Closing the gate behind me I was met with quite a wonderful sight, for it had snowed quite heavily overnight and my walk to the train station was through a little white winter wonderland. With the snow thick and yet untouched by human feet, it felt solid enough for me to be able to maintain my normal quick walking pace. I was no earlier that morning than I normally was but the streets seemed quieter, as if the cold night was causing people to be reluctant to move from their beds. Even the main roads of that part of the city were quiet, not filled with their normal commuting traffic. Climbing the steps to the platform at Polsloe Bridge I found myself standing with two women who explained that they were actually waiting for the train travelling in the opposite direction heading for Exmouth; this normally arrived twenty minutes before mine, which on a normal day would therefore have been a good few minutes before I even got to the platform. The only sign of life on the railway was the distant sight of brake lights from the even earlier train which was not moving. As we stood there in the crisp chill of the quite early morn we were joined one at a time by two more individuals, one of whom was gentleman of similar height and build as myself and who had carried a mountain bike up the stairs to the platform so that when he got to his terminal train station he could ride the rest of the journey to his chosen destination. This was something I had often contemplated the merits of doing, deciding that the proximity of both Rosie's house and my university campus to their closest respective stations made the use of my bike feel a little like overkill, especially as walking was, from a time perspective, a perfectly viable means of making the journey. The next individual to add themselves to the population of Polsloe Bridge that morning was a member of staff for the train operator; he was an inch or so taller than myself and looked to hold a little more weight around the midsection, but dressed in such a way as to conceal this by appropriate use of his uniform garments, and his shoes were well-kept, clean and polished. As he stood there surveying the situation he had found himself in, I noticed his hair was thick jet black, and slicked back tight to the contours of his head before falling down his back in an impressively long and shiny ponytail. Some time passed and our member of railway staff began to become as frustrated by the lack of train as the rest of us, however he was an inside man so to speak; he soon revealed his pocket aces, his hidden answer to our situation. Reaching into his jacket pocket, he produced his mobile phone. He thumbed through his contact list and then he began to make a call. It transpired that the call he was making was through to someone of authority within the local rail network, out of respect for his privacy I tried my best to put some distance between myself and him and not listen in on his conversation. However on such a short platform in such quiet and still conditions this proved quite a difficult task. After his call was over he donned a high-vis tabard and, warning us not to follow him, strolled off the sloping end of the platform in the direction of the brake lights and stationary train a few hundred yards up the line, disappearing into the night as he did so. A couple of minutes passed till he returned from the darkness, striding back up the slope of the platform to inform us all that he had been able to pull a few strings while on the phone and that as he was needed at St David's. The train up ahead would in a few moments be reversing back to the platform to pick us up before slowly edging its way to St David's. At the point of my arrival at university some half hour late I got to my lecture room in time to catch the last student from my group packing up their things and heading for the library as it has transpired that I was not the only one to have had my day's journey plans torn to pieces by the weather over the previous night - our lecturer had not been able to make it in for our lecture. I spent the majority of the remaining day eating, something I have found I am incredibly efficient at.

Chapter Ten
Seat Numbers, Where the Hell Is My Seat?

One of the most fundamental aspects of public transport is the need to acquire a ticket for your travel. I know a great number of people who will admit to keeping tickets as mementos of particular important journeys. Purchasing tickets can be a bit of a nightmare. From the confusion of the timetables and price structure to the plain ignorance of some of the staff that you may eventually have to deal with, ticket sales can be one of the worst experiences that comes from public transport, which why I the enjoy digital alternatives such the ticket websites and automated ticket machines. They are fast, simple and do not require any human interaction. I have to be honest here as well as to say that the problems of traditional ticket sales have not always been the problem of the ticket sale operator; sometimes my own lack of focus has caused unnecessary disruption. Which is all the more reason for the shiny little box on the platform. I can't offend it because it's 6:07 in the morning and the Earl Grey and Weetabix haven't kicked in yet. Most train company websites have also taken this on board and now allow for the purchase and even printing of tickets direct from the comfort of your own home. This is in some ways even better; I can even ignore the queue of people I would normally have to stand in and attempt not to offend while waiting for my turn to purchase the ticket from the machine that stops me from offending people. These new methods of unsupervised self-ticketing do come with their own issues. One example of a problem with self-ticketing comes from the requirement of multiple tickets for a journey that occurs in several isolated stages. The ticket machine on the station platform always assumes departure and return directly to the station from which the ticket is being purchased. Now I admit this does seem logical and for the majority of users this would not cause any form of a problem. For a select few such as myself, for example, who wanted to go from say, Barnstaple to the branch line southeast of Exeter on the 5th then from the branch line south east of Exeter back across the city and then on to Bristol via a mainline service on the 6th, followed by Bristol all the way back to Barnstaple on the 6th as well, only this time via Exeter's mainline station only, this often involved two sets of open return tickets or in some cases a combination of return and single tickets filling my wallet with hundreds of little orange and white cardboard slips. Ticket in hand, you then must shuffle up and down the carriage or platform looking for the corresponding seat number hoping that you won't find some small child or comatose drunk in residence.

The advent of some websites allow you not only to purchase a ticket but also to go as far as requesting a specific seat reservation brings the potential for some hilarious confusion in the carriage. On some of these websites you can specify if you require a seat close to a toilet or at a table. Reservations for table seats have given me some of the most hilarious sights I have had the opportunity of witnessing on public transport. I must point out that I don't often reserve seats myself and to my knowledge have never specifically requested a seat at a table. I however have come to the conclusion that for the most part only two groups of people request this service. The most frequent being the professional type such as the corporate lawyer, architect or head teacher. The second group of rail users in need of the extra space afforded by the table seats are single mothers, who often seem too young or ill-prepared for them to be left in charge of anything, even if it did eject itself from their body after nine months of incubation. I enjoy sitting directly behind the table group. Observing those who chose to sit there, the morning train to Bristol often produced great entertainment by doing this. Countless individuals board the train at different stations with tickets and reserve slips for table seats carrying arms full of paperwork to spread out in a space-commanding fashion, only to find they have to share with like-minded individuals. For example, at the three stations Exeter, Tiverton and Taunton, by the time the train reaches Bristol Temple Meads, there are four frustrated professionals all with mixed up or missing drawings or drafts of work they require for their next meeting.

Chapter Eleven
Delayed Train = Winner!
Have I Gone Mad?

Delayed trains and/or buses are, most of the time, one of the biggest problems with public transport. For example, if your journey is complex, or it involves a number of sequential connections, often with little time between alighting one vehicle. Before having to board another, the error caused by one arriving late can have catastrophic effects such as making the rest of the onward journey sometimes pointless and void. There are the occasional instances when a delayed train can be a fortunate or serendipitous occurrence, for example, when the time it takes to get to the station from your original starting location would normally leave mere moments of leeway to allow for unforeseen traffic or other such complication. This is the one and only time that a train being delayed was of advantage to me instead of a hindrance. On my way back to Bristol Parkway from UWE I came across a young boy who was about to be set upon by a couple of bullies. Similar to the moment I met the man who was lost on his way to Southmead Hospital, I found myself faced with a dilemma - did I a) do the honourable action of stepping in, protecting the boy from his violent school peers, meaning that I would miss my train? Or b), did I ignore my moral compass and walk on by to catch my train leaving him to his own fate, whatever that may have been? Having a strong sense of moral decency and belief in the virtues of pure intentions I walked over and gently pulled the two aggressive youngsters off the clearly timid little boy to which he looked up and thanked me before darting off as quickly as his legs could take him. The two early teenage boys turned around to face me. The alpha male of the pair took a swing at me first but missed with his partner following him like pack animal. The second punch connected with my stomach but was so weak I could barely register it. Not being an aggressive man and understanding they were still only minors compared to the fully grown adult male that I was, I refused to retaliate, instead walking straight through between them. I straightened my clothing and continued my journey to Parkway, completely ignoring the insults they shouted. Upon getting to the station I was delighted to hear the announcement that the train I had originally planned to get had been delayed due to signalling problems further up the line north of Bristol and had not actually arrived yet, so following my inbuilt moral compass had not had any lasting effect on my journey.

Chapter Twelve
Appearances Really Do Matter

If there is only one item of truly useful information that can be gained from a year spent analysing public transport I believe that I have been fortunate enough to learn it. Now that I have been blessed with knowledge I see myself as duty bound to pass it on and enlighten people so that others who find themselves in the same or similar situations can more quickly adopt this and benefit from what it suggests about the consciousness of the general public and how we perceive and then react to the other individuals in our environment. I like to think of myself generally as polite and friendly. Although, I am not much of an overt extrovert and as a rule I have a dislike of those individuals who feel it necessary to push themselves on people. I hope however that I come across as pleasant and approachable when in social situations. Like most other forms of transport trains are a situation where the driver is often best left alone to concentrate on the potentially dangerous task of keeping control of the tonne or more commonly multiple of metal he or she happens to be piloting. With no real function apart from benefitting from the service of transportation point to point and paying whatever is due for this service, the passengers are left to occupy themselves and/or each other during the trip. Now most modern vehicles are installed with a radio, internet and/or television. Some are so quiet and comfortable that sleep is an option, as is to view the world as it speeds by. A lecturer of mine once admitted that she found train journeys an excellent place to do marking of our essays which was something I had already guessed due similarities between marking an essay and writing an essay to be marked; as both jobs require similar skills and use of the same techniques, it seemed logical to assume they could be accomplished in similar if not the same sorts of environments. Now every lecturer and for that matter every student, has their own personal working style. To complement that style everyone has to find a preferred working environment. For some, it's found in the calm quiet seclusion of the library late at night, while for others it's used as a distraction from the overcrowded train or bus on the way home; as for myself I fall somewhere in between these two extremes. This is due to me being too interested in the world around me. A demon exorcised by making critical observations of my environment. This does not leave me able to concentrate on the task of producing an accurate technical report or the rebuttal of a well-researched factual essay. My attempts at quiet work in the corner of the library similarly failed to produce the desired effect. Often these attempts at hard work in such a peaceful environment have ended with me, being found by someone, having fallen asleep on a textbook or worse, my laptop, and in one extreme case with my head in my lunch container of spaghetti carbonara. The problem with working in the library was the fact that it was so quiet and peaceful that all I felt able to do was drift off to sleep. After several of these endeavours earlier on in my university life I found the secret element with made concentrating in most environments possible, this was a small amount of music. Once armed with headphones, everywhere became a possible workstation. This fact then gave rise to a dilemma of its own. For you see, I could quite happily sit on the train, laptop in hand, punching out an essay as the world rolled by to the soundtrack supplied by my mp3 player almost completely ignoring the other passengers on the train. This state of hard work however took a short while to settle into, however, so I found myself with the problem keeping the seat next to me empty until the point that I was too lost in my work for anyone who sat next to me to be of interest to me and attempt to engage me in conversation. I needed to find some way of deterring people without being outright rude by placing my baggage in the adjacent seat. I began by consulting some friends who had knowledge of psychology and when that did not reveal a rock solid answer I began to experiment with the idea that seemed to most likely to produce the desired result. The result I wished to achieve was when first sitting on the train before I had even decided to start typing people could look at me and decide not to sit next to me, but by the same measure not be so put off by the idea of spending time with me that should I decide not to work, that I didn't have to spend the whole journey sitting alone. The variable I was going to try and monitor was my own appearance. I used different combinations of my wardrobe and looked for any patterns of behaviour that they induced in other people. The only real downfall with this experiment was that the other passengers who had witnessed my different outfits were not always constant. I mean getting the same trains at the same times each week meant that there was a core of people who were on the train almost every time but then there was the unknown factor of the people who were only occasional or only going be on the train with me the once. The presence of these people changed the demographic, the cultural dynamic of the train, potentially putting a selection pressure on my results, making the data skewed in one way or another. This could have occurred because their presence was affecting the behaviour of the other passengers as a group. Over the months I tried clothing from full grey pinstriped business suits through to skin-tight fluorescent cycling tops and shorts while taking measurements of the time I had someone sitting next to me when wearing each and compared this to how busy the train was at the time to see if there was any discernible pattern in people's attraction or repulsion towards my appearance. Some of my results were easy to explain but mostly the two outright extremes were somewhat unexpected by my initial hypothesis. Depending on your outlook on life and your requirements for either company or space on your train journey I do hope you find the following information useful. At the bottom of the scale, in terms of seeming to be the least socially acceptable item, was the black or dark blue hoody. Possibly due to links within the media to anti-social behaviour orders (ASBOs) this item of clothing was avoided at all costs, even on very busy trains and so scored the shortest 'companion time' of all. Even other people in hoodies did not want to sit next to me and so now you too know the single item of clothing most likely to get you left alone on public transport. What is even more shocking is that the negative effects of the hoody overpowered any positive energy of anything it was worn with. The cycling gear often produced confusion on first sight, this was less so if the bike was or had been in view. Once they had had the chance to digest the image and take on board any visible brand labels or charity references the cycling gear began gaining quite a length of companion time as people asked questions and engaged me in conversation about rides I was planning to take on, the training I had done, technical queries regarding my choice of bike, equipment as well as diet and lifestyle. So much was the apparent interest in my hobby that I became well practiced in answering the commonly reoccurring questions. Questions like how long had I been a cyclist? Typically these were asked by non-cyclists, to which my standard answer was "less than a year". Another question typically fielded by those whose knowledge of the sport was simply that of a by-standing witness was classically, how did I come to get involved, how did it start for me? To this my given answer was often along the line of; I wanted to get fitter and could remember that I used to enjoy cycling as young boy. I often followed this up by pointing out that I also wanted to do something for charity and so signed myself up to a cycling challenge the same day I purchased my bike, but more on that later. The idea being that I had a goal in terms of fitness level and a deadline by which it had to be attained, in addition to this I had the encouragement of knowing that no matter how hard and painful the training, I was doing something that not only helped me but also helped those less able or as fortunate as myself. For these reasons, I enjoyed being questioned about my hobby however I did not want to become famous as the cycling nutcase who goes for train rides all over the country. I'm sure this is similar to the headline that would have been printed had cycling clothing been my only attire worn on my train journeys. Therefore my cycling gear was also mixed and mismatched with normal T-shirts, shirts, jackets, shorts and jeans to be able to continue my psychology experiment. All normal everyday casual wear seemed to amass similar amounts of companion time, being hindered by the addition of a hoody or enhanced by the presence of cycling items as previously explained. The category that scored the highest was by far my formal wear. For example, the highest scoring single item turned to be a surprise to me - my Marks and Spencer's tailored long black woollen overcoat. At the original full price of over two hundred pounds it is one of the most expensive items in my normal, non-suit wardrobe. As it is finished with large black buttons, and has a silky pearlescent dark green interior lining, it carries a timelessly simple elegance. A close friend of mine often refers to it as my MIB or Men in Black jacket stating references to the actor Will Smith. Being long haired and bearded with blue eyes, only five foot eleven and of English ancestry I am never going entertain the notion that there is any form of physical resemblance between myself and Will Smith. Nonetheless the addition of my jacket to any outfit seems to make me a prime target for people looking for someone to sit next to. I am unsure at this point whether this in due to a material image of expensive tastes meaning money to waste, or that it projects an image of authority and office, therefore equalling safety and security. My best guess, I would say that there is no one single answer for the jacket's apparent effect. Only that it's probable that elements of both the given possibilities have some sort of bearing on each individual's assessment of me. In most cases, this leads to the decision being made, that I would be pleasant to sit by for an hour or so. As you have probably guessed, while wearing the jacket I had plenty of opportunity to be social but not much essay writing. Welcome to enlightenment, go forth and enjoy any train journey like never before, as you have now been informed of my method for increasing the likelihood of either being completely ignored or approached while sitting quietly on the train.

Chapter Thirteen
Trains for Recreation? Seriously Here, I Haven't Gone Bonkers

I hope now to explain a situation of total triumph where I believe the train line between Barnstaple and Exeter is really useful, in fact, my preferred mode of transport. My friends and I enjoy a good game of rugby. A couple of us have played a little at times in our lives. On the east side of Exeter is Sandy Park Stadium, home of one of the most successful rugby union teams in the far south west of England, the Exeter Chiefs. Five minutes' walk from the entrance to the ground is the very edge of the city's suburbs and the train platform of Digby and Sowton. The same train that travels between Barnstaple and Exeter intermittently carries on further through Exeter on to another branch line which takes it past Digby and Sowton and on through the east Devon countryside in the direction of the coastal town of Exmouth on the south coast. This fact has previously made for a number of good days out, making my way into Barnstaple to meet up with a group of friends before jumping on a train together to meet Rosie in Exeter for a spot of lunch and a couple of pints of cider, before catching the next train through to Digby in time to watch the Chiefs smash in to their opponents as part of eighty minutes of tough physical sporting excitement known commonly as the game of rugby union. Once the game had finished I was left with two options, either return to Rosie's student accommodation with her for the evening or end the day back on the train to Barnstaple, in time to get ready for a night out back at home. Short of hiring a people carrier/minibus and either a chauffeur or designating one of us who could drive to do so the train is the only method of transport where a day such as this can be had, accompanied with the sharing of a few bottles of cider while in transit, not forgetting a half time hog roast bap with crackling and apple sauce, which has become a staple of our match day diets.

Chapter Fourteen
The Luck of the Irish or Not, As the Case May Be

Only a few days after my final exams, I was fortunate enough to be on my way to an international conference on microbiology run by a learned society for which I am a member of. The venue and host city for that particular year's conference was the wonderfully comfortable Clontarf Castle Hotel in the historic and interesting Irish city of Dublin, on the east coast of the emerald Republic of Ireland. To attend this event I had to travel on yet another form of transport - an aeroplane. I do not wish to disappoint anyone but I don't have much to say on the subject of skyward travel. Depending on the operator, airports with both departing and arriving commercial aviation can be plagued with similar problems of price, timetabling, security and seating as train travel and bus transport. On the morning of the conference my family were kind enough to give me a lift to Bristol International Airport for my early morning flight to the emerald isle to negate the expense of airport parking. At the other end of my completely uneventful and only mildly uncomfortable one hour budget flight I had to find a way across the city from the airport to the hosting hotel. The society had provided me with a rough map outlining the geographical separation and an indication of both journey time as well as price in a taxi. None of which was actually of much use as I had already chosen to travel by combination of bus and walking, paying thanks to you, the road atlas I keep in my car, preventing me from ever becoming lost. I did this in the hope of learning a little about the geography and an understanding of my surroundings. This plan paid off. Later on that week the other younger members of the society and I got the opportunity to explore the Dublin night life. Having made my own explorative way to the conference venue I was now confident in my ability to make my way safely back to the hotel should I have been split off from everyone I was enjoying an evening out with. Contingency planning aside I wasn't separated from the group after a night spent in Temple Bar, sampling the odd pint of Guinness and several Irish attempts at cider coming strictly to the firm conclusion that they were quite drinkable and a good option for a novice cider drinker - I was no novice, so found no match for the rugged flavour of my local favourite from a small Devon cider farm on the edge of Exmoor, or as delightful and easy to enjoy as Healey's Classic Reserve from Penhallow in Cornwall.

Chapter Fifteen

The Day That the Car and Train Were Both Replaced By Two Wheels and a Set of Pedals as My Main Mode of Transport

At the beginning of her second year I wished to test the condition of my mental and physical resolve and so attempted to cycle from my home to Rosie's university accommodation. At the time I was somewhat unfit but could remember in great detail the time before my driving licence during my early to mid-teenage years when I used to regularly cycle over to the beach at Woolacombe or Croyde and how much fun I had doing so. The bike I owned and very rarely looked at by this point in my mid-twenties was a superbly comfortable but astonishingly heavy steel framed mountain bike with full suspension front and rear, very much an off roader not designed for the country roads I was going to be taking it on, but off I went, backpack and all. This being my first attempt was of only mild success. I managed to complete the journey but this was completed in a rather embarrassing time being only able to average a pitiful nine miles an hour. This I protested was mainly due to the bike's dual suspension set up which may have been comfortable to sit on, but did a good job of sapping almost all of the energy out of each stroke of the pedals. It was clear to me that the bike was not built for road cycling such a distance therefore making it redundant for my needs at the time, and so the following weekend the bike was put up for sale. A couple of long winter months passed and the New Year was upon us and with it a renewed enthusiasm for improving myself in every manner possible. This renewed feeling of the need for self-improvement focused itself on the idea of becoming an amateur road cyclist in the name of a charitable cause. Having spent days trawling the internet for information I finally settled on the idea of taking part in the ACTION MEDICAL RESEARCH London to Paris four day tour through south east England and northern France. That very same day I put my money where my mouth was, signed up to the event and also purchased an entry level aluminium road bike.

The bike I chose in my haste was a brand new current model, a white Barossa Monza. Costing a little less than two hundred pounds it was among the cheapest of the bikes I had looked at, but it had an underdog feel to the specification that seemed to say that it was very basic but had all that was required to do a good job and nothing more. A sort of philosophy of minimum outlay producing maximum impressive effect; a policy that I seem naturally accustomed to. After waiting a couple of weeks for delivery it finally arrived all fully assembled and ready for action. Starting slowly with the occasional outing for half hour to an hour or so I found myself enjoying the fact that this bike was much more manoeuvrable, far easier to control and I could pick up speed more rapidly than I had been able to on the sluggish mountain bike. Soon I settled in to a more structured schedule of cycling three times a week, slowly increasing my travelling speed and distance as I canvassed the local area for sponsors. The more used to being on the bike I became the more I found myself planning progressively longer rides. With spring in full flight my weeks involved two twenty-five mile rides and one forty or fifty mile trip. Friends and family became very comfortable with the sight of my brightly coloured cycling clothing and I purchased a pannier rack and bags with the intention of increasing my regular range to even longer a distance. This new method of transport was not without its drawbacks and limitations. The two biggest problems I encountered during the initial months of owning the new bike were as follows:

The discomfort felt riding the bike. This was more apparent than it had been with the mountain bike for a number of reasons. The bike was a stiff frame with no form of suspension, the saddle was smaller and of a more streamlined shape. The handlebars were drop over loops, requiring you to sit leaning over to the front of the bike. And finally the tyres were narrow and pressurised to just over one hundred psi. These factors combined cause any irregularity in road surface to be felt.

My second issue to overcome was the loneliness. I could always arrange to meet my friends at some destination but found it difficult to convince any of my friends to actually join me en route if I was planning to cover any real distance. On the occasions when people did join me I felt handicapped by the fact that I needed to reduce my pace to one which my comrades could maintain.

With the end of the academic year looming on the horizon I was given the opportunity to visit Rosie over a weekend for one of her housemate's birthdays. This worked wonderfully as it gave me a chance to once again test my fitness and attempt cycling between my home and her house down the by now very familiar Crediton Road. Once I was fully loaded with all that I required shoehorned in to my pannier rack, off I set via Barnstaple and Crediton to Exeter. I was pleased to find that the combination of the correct bike and a fair training program had paid off as I was able to average more than double the speed of my previous attempt at that route, getting in to Exeter at a sensible time in the day. Again this ended up in a wonderful evening with Rosie and her friends. It was at this point I found myself thinking that I no longer had to rely on the expense of cars or the infrequency of trains; I felt that I could perfectly happily make my way anywhere with just the bike and my panniers full of stuff. The following morning after our customary goodbyes and feeling somewhat tired I cycled back from Rosie's as far a St David's train station on the other side of the city centre with the intention of catching a train back to Barnstaple and cycling the last few miles of the journey home. Unfortunately upon arrival at St David's I was informed that there was no direct train due to a problem with the line just outside Exeter and that I needed to go outside as there was alternative road transport being provided to take people as far as Crediton. After speaking to a member of staff by the bus stop I was informed that a bus was on its way to collect anyone bound for Barnstaple and deliver them to Crediton to catch the connecting train. He unfortunately also informed me that this may in fact be a coach which would have difficulties taking my bike. I spent the next few minutes deciding whether or not I had the energy and time to cycle to Crediton and catch the train myself when the bus swept into view and to my relief was capable of taking my bike aboard. I returned home with a plan. I had to prepare for Rosie's return from university for the summer.

Chapter Sixteen
Rosie's Birthday

It was to be Rosie's 21st birthday over that summer, a time that I was most excited about as I very much enjoy parties, especially organising momentous important social events. I wished to make sure it was a big event as fitting of the grandeur of the occasion being celebrated; this fact seemed to anger Rosie somewhat. While out doing a spot of cycle training for my oncoming challenge I came across a herd of escaped cattle which in a roundabout way convinced me that a BBQ would be the best answer to the question of food. That and the fact that I had recently acquired a sizable beast of a gas and/or coal fired BBQ. I pedalled homeward to send texts and emails to as many of her friends as I was able to directly contact in the hope that the message would be disseminated through groups. Much to my dismay many of Rosie's university friends whom I was able to contact directly could not attend and even more disheartening, most even failed to respond at all. On a more positive note almost all of her close school friends responded quickly and I soon had a nice but relatively short list of attendees and an almost equally long list of help being offered.

With the date steadily approaching I began to decide more definitively about the food I could offer. Now I enjoy cooking, most of all I enjoy experimenting with interesting foods and/or technical cooking methods. After closer inspection of the monster BBQ that took up a large amount of the patio space outside my flat, I came to the conclusion that the answer was in fact to set up the rotating spit attachment to attempt a sort of hog roast affair.

Fortunately for me at this point, my brother and I have both worked for and since remained on good speaking terms with Mr Mike Turton, one of the town's local butchers. I have to say a big thank you to him and his skills for cutting and preparing an enormous section of pig for me to collect and then struggle to transport home the day before the event. Now when I say enormous I mean it, all 30 plus kg of it. Having never tried to cook a spit roast before I decided that simplicity was probably going to be the key to success, so once Rosie had gone to work in the morning I retrieved the epic looking chunk of pork from its cool hiding place, lit the BBQ and set the meat slowly turning on its spike. A small amount of time was spent preparing a couple of homemade sauces such as a thick honey and lemon mustard glaze, which I regularly coated the joint with, gently brushing it over the turning meat. I then created some equally interesting spiced apple sauce. With the meat rotating slowly and the sauce gently chilling in the fridge, I turned my attention to another of my party passions: cocktails. Having consulted my recipe books I decided on an impressively extensive but perfectly accomplishable list of interesting drinks. I spoke with my mother who had offered to put on her baking cap and provide a birthday cake. Feeling like things were well in hand I took a quick trip down to the shops for alcoholic ingredients, fruit juices, soft drinks, potatoes, salads and breads to accompany my manly meat. Hours later the cooked pork was placed in a warm oven to rest out of sight, and the cocktails and spirits were gently cooling in the fridge or sitting patiently in my drinks cabinet just in time for Rosie to return from her long day at work aware that she had only an hour to relax and chill out before her friends were coming over to celebrate her birthday, but thankfully unaware of the expense, time, and effort that had gone into what I hoped would be yet another addition to the list of momentous parties at the Elwell residence.

Chapter Seventeen

Heading for Paris: A Week in the Life of This Charity Cyclist

With Rosie's Birthday celebrations having passed a month previous my attention focused firmly on my epic six days filled with a great many highs and very few lows as I made my journey to Paris and back for charity. I must start by explaining that the official commencement of my adventure was in fact to begin the morning after my graduation day. Now this, I thought, wouldn't on the face of it be much of a problem. How wrong I was. Tuesday the nineteenth of July started very early with the sight of my favourite dark grey pinstriped business suit. Unfortunately I wasn't wearing it yet, instead I was slipping in to much more casual clothing and placing the suit in my Carlton international hanging garment carrier for use later. The day of my graduation was to be an incredible day but also a logistical nightmare. After breakfast I made a last check of my things before wheeling my bike out to the road. Due to the tight schedule I needed to keep to, I was to be picked up from home by my father's friend Neil who at the time owned a small and rather battered, but nonetheless serviceable and quite reliable little Vauxhall

Combi van. My bicycle, suit carrier and overnight bag of all my equipment, clothes, and toiletries I had prepared for the days ahead were loaded into the little red van. Neil had been instructed to take me to meet my parents at Barnstaple train station as the three of us, mother, father and I had tickets for the next train to Exeter so that we could catch a connecting train up to Bristol Temple Meads. The platform at Barnstaple was far busier at this morning hour than the evening train I was accustomed to getting. Sitting on the platform munching my way through a sausage and bacon bap from the station master's café, one of the few exceptions to my earlier rant about train station food outlets, I noticed that a friend of mine, Joel Cooper, was waiting for the same train. Joel was a charismatic journalist for one of the local papers, who was being sent up to the Buckingham Palace garden party to cover the event, and for that matter looked quite smart in a suit, more fitting of my usual style, and so looked far removed from me and my cycling shorts. After explaining the reason for my baggage, not to mention why I was dressed the way I was, it was time to board the train. After leaving the bike in a designated area close to the carriage doors, I surveyed the carriage. As the train was crowded I quickly opted for the seat next to Joel, which was luckily opposite my parents. Following a basically uneventful journey to Exeter spent mainly discussing professional road cyclists as well as other cycling tours I would be interested in taking part in, we arrived at Exeter where Joel and I parted company. Once my family and I made it to Temple Meads station in Bristol I made haste with exchanging my cycling gear for my suit so that we could proceed across town to College Green and attend the formal celebration of my graduation from my undergraduate degree.

After several hours of clapping and cheering for fellow graduates, lots of hand shaking, posing for photos and kind words from my lecturers it was time for me to de-gown, remove the suit and slip back in to my cycling Lycra. Upon returning to Temple Meads I bid my family farewell as they and my suit, were returning home to Devon where as I was in fact taking a train travelling in the opposite direction heading for London. My destination for that evening being the Aerodrome Hotel in Croydon, the train journey was completely uneventful bar the occasional question about my outfit. Once I had stepped out of the station in West Croydon I began to ask for directions to or a map showing the location of the hotel. Cycling through Croydon was quite a horrible experience, reminding me why I prefer cycling and driving in the countryside, over the seemingly dirty, grey, and chaotic wasteland which stereotypes deprived areas of big cities. After struggling along with my overnight suitcase strapped over the top of my panniers with bungee cords, I finally made it through the landscape of burned out cars and steel fronted abandoned shops to the hotel. From the exterior the Aerodrome Hotel looked very art deco in styling and looked as though it may have been a functional part of a small airfield at some point in its history. Bringing my bike to a stop I dismounted in the car park and pushed the bike over to the reception entrance. I chained my bike to a pillar next to the doors when two women sauntered out of the double doors of the hotel to get something from a car which was parked behind me on the other side of the car park. Pulling open both of the doors I stepped inside the reception letting both doors slam shut behind me. A method I often use to make sure my arrival has been noticed in most places I go, living by the idea that if there are two doors, use both of them. The reception desk was to the left of the door and standing in the lobby next to the lifts was a large A frame notice board explaining that the ride would be departing from the car park at seven the following morning and that the hotel had not only provided an extra early service of breakfast for us which started at six, but had also turned one of the ground floor conference rooms in to a secure overnight storage for our bikes. I walked over to the desk and gave my details to the receptionist who handed me my room key and directions to my room before calling for another member of staff to show me to the bike store as it remained locked between people dropping off their wheels.

As I waited for said staff member I turned to be greeted by the sight of a beautiful young blonde woman striding up to the desk to ask the receptionist a question. I noticed that her clothing was of a sporty nature and that she was wearing running shoe style trainers. From this I guessed she was one of the riders I would be cycling the route to Paris with; once her query has been answered by the receptionist I introduced myself and asked if she was indeed going to be partaking in this little cycling adventure. To this she answered yes and introduced herself as Kate, a journalist who worked for a cycling magazine in Bath, for whom she was being sent on this ride to cover it for her first major article to be published in an up and coming issue of the magazine. Over the following few minutes we spoke about cycling and our respective backgrounds, the more I looked upon her beauty the more I was reminded of how beautiful my dearest Rosie was to me and how Kate's fiancée must have felt as wonderful as I did. With the arrival of the hotel staff member I had been waiting for, Kate and I parted ways.

Wheeling my bike through the corridors of the hotel I was taken to the bike store which was normally one of the hotel's meeting rooms that had its furniture stacked up against one wall to make room for what must have been thousands if not a hundred thousand pounds worth of push bikes of all colours. Finding space near a curtain covered window I placed my bike among its far more expensive brethren before making my way up the four floors to my room to phone Rosie and get ready for bed as it was close to eleven o'clock before I even had my key in the door.

Chapter Eighteen

Day One: London to Dover and Beyond

The day began just before six a.m. after waking up in my relatively cold and lonely hotel room. I proceeded to start my day off with a nice and gentle cool to lukewarm shower and a good rub down with anti-chafing cream before squeezing my larger the your average cyclist's frame into a pair of cycling shorts followed by an extremely bright neon yellow long sleeved hi-visibility top. Slipping on a pair of my favourite flip flops I proceeded downstairs to the hotel's restaurant with the intention of having as big a breakfast as possible to set me up for the day ahead using the concept that food is fuel and I was going to require a lot.

Walking boldly in to the room, I noted quickly the few people who had been even earlier than me, as they had almost finished their breakfast by the time of my arrival. After giving my name and room number at the desk I was shown to a table and asked if I would prefer a coffee or tea to which my standard response is always tea. I took a moment to survey the available options before deciding that it was best I begin with a bowl of corn flakes with a banana and some orange juice, then let that settle before attacking the cooked breakfast hot plate. As I sat there serenely munching on my corn flakes I drifted off, paying more attention to the view of the hotel's slowly filling car park and less to the dawdling pace that the other guests were appearing for breakfast. So much was I locked in my own little world that I almost failed to notice I was about to be joined for the rest of my morning meal. My first guest was a tall Scottish man whose physical shape was more like that of an aging professional cyclist, he was easily more than a stone lighter in weight then myself, even though he stood a clear couple of inches taller. He wore the team wear of his local cycling organization tight over small but well defined muscle groups. Sitting down to his breakfast he opened communication by asking what I had done previously in terms of cycling events, and how did I feel about the challenges ahead? To this I answered as I had when Kate had put the same line of questioning to me. In a humble manner, I felt I could complete it but I did not feel I would do so in spectacular fashion. Turning the focus away from me I politely questioned my table companion on the same matters. As I perched there paying attention across the table, it was clear he was far more experienced at road cycling events than I and was, as I first guessed, in very good physical shape for a man of his years. It was at this point I heard the little voice in my head complain that the hot food counter was waiting; my eyes darted over in the direction of the aforementioned food before tracking back across the room. I subconsciously calculated the probability of ending up stuck in a queue. Before I was able to rise to my feet, my attention was taken by the image of Kate who had decided to join the Scottish fellow and me for her breakfast. Following a few pleasantries I made haste for the bacon, eggs and such. Returning to our table, I made apologies for the somewhat ungracious manner in which I had crossed the room. I had done so with the swagger of Dean Martin with a sausage hanging from my mouth like some sort of pork meat Cuban cigar. While finishing breakfast together we spoke about university life as

Kate studied a post grad course at UWE and so knew my campus well.

After breakfast I rushed back to my room to collect my luggage ready to check out. Back in the hotel entrance my next port of call was the bike room to collect my chariot. Leaving the hotel with my ride the car park was full, with loads of cyclists all centring around a lorry. Scooting up closer for a better view, the 7.5 tonne van was in fact the check-in station for the start of the event. After giving my name, number and overnight bag in to the officials, I began to mingle with my fellow cyclists, as the idea of four days of cycling alone and spending my evenings alone was not exactly my idea of a perfect trip. It wasn't long until my friendly nature and slightly mad dress sense attracted people to me. The first person to approach me was the even crazier dressed James Everson, who had used his numerous business contacts to fill his sponsorship quota by promising to use himself as a mobile billboard and selling off sections of his cycling jersey to the highest bidders to use as advertising as he cycled during his training, and finally while travelling the country roads of the extreme south east of England and northern France. Now it has to be said that my clothing was eye catching due to the eye catching colours and highly reflective silver and black sections of aerated breathable material; James' cycling attire was a more tonal red and white affair that was covered in logos and business product names of James' seemingly massive contact list. To top this off he had a mad pair of sunglasses which he was attempting to wear simultaneously with a sports visor. It was also clear on inspection of his bike that he was not only a keen cyclist well practiced at events such as this, he was also a man sensibly well off, and seemingly self-made. After posing together for several photographs, James revealed yet another memorable aspect of his character which over the following few days made me admire him even more, something of a hat tip to any extreme sports or adventure enthusiasts reading this, the man had a genuine GoPro helmet cam. James then proceeded to inspect my equipment, commenting that he admired my back-to-basics, simple and cost-effective bike that cost around one fifth of the price of his, and I quote the man himself "looked perfectly capable of the task at hand." He also made a point of witnessing that I was the only person to be travelling with a full symmetrical 35L set of pannier bags.

Discussing cycling and preparation for the event it was clear that in terms of length of time previously spent in the saddle, James outclassed me by years however he gave me some small words of encouragement, saying that the training I had done over the months leading up to that day would prove to have been adequate and that the ride was simple and should only pose a mild to medium challenge.

The next person to catch my eye was again the Scotsman I had shared the breakfast table with. We only briefly exchanged gestures of good luck before the event's team called us all in to huddle closer together at the back of the van so they could formally introduce themselves and give us the planned running order for the day ahead. During this they also explained that for the next four days our maps and sat navigation systems would only be need in emergencies as the whole route was mapped out using low tech but highly effective neon orange flag shaped signs. We were then instructed to turn one hundred and eighty degrees before shuffling in formation towards the mouth of the car park. Being that I was one of the last to arrive at the van I was then part of the first wave to reach the car park exit, where we stood for what felt like forever until the impatient grumbling from behind me was broken with the crack of a starting pistol! Awkwardly the crowd around me still seemed reluctant to move as if held back by some invisible tether. With the hundred plus riders twitching their cleats, the reason for this wait however was the volume of traffic that surged down the road past the hotel entrance, stopping us from safely exiting the car park en masse. As soon as a break in the line of oncoming cars was visible the group began to inch out on to the road and merge with the traffic. Moments later we were all underway, and I found myself once again in the company of Kate who was gently complaining about the idea of not having satellite navigation to follow. Something I explained did not faze me due to my perfectly adequate map reading skills and incredible natural sense of direction, honestly it's like I have a north seeking magnet built into my backside. The area we were cycling through was not however well signposted as is common at the point that the city mixes in to the suburbs, which as we cycled seemed to be becoming more of an inner city setting and therefore more built up and crowded. It was clear to me that I was not going to be able to comfortably keep pace with Kate as her natural cycling speed was a fair bit quicker than mine, so I bid her farewell as she went in pursuit of one of the more semipro cyclists at the head of the group for an interview. Our first big challenge came within a mere two miles from the start line, in the shape of a very long and somewhat unrelenting hill climb. Now my hill climbing was definitely an area where my cycling lacked performance. As I felt myself slowing down and losing cadence, I reached for the wine gums I had hidden in the centre pocket of my fluorescent cycling jersey. This simple fruit flavoured gelatine was not enough to sustain me, and only a few yards farther up the hill I was beginning to feel strained. An element of panic and doubt washed over me, questioning my ability to complete what I had committed myself to. I then saw two wondrous sights; the first was the perfectly average sight of a postman walking down the hill whistling, followed by the sight of James Everson drawing up level with me. As he did so, he gave me a small pep talk - unfortunately the exact words escape my memory - but it has to be said that whatever he said, was enough to put the steel back in my spine; momentarily calm the lactic acid building up in my quadriceps; and see me power though to the summit at a slow, but steady rhythmic pace. As the road flattened, and the numbness in my legs and chest lessened, I glanced far off in the horizon to the joyous sight of some fifty cyclists powering along in the morning sun. Glancing over my shoulder, I was delighted to behold the sight of approximately a further fifty cyclists about to mount the summit behind me. Accelerating in pace to a more sensible seventeen miles per hour, the countryside began to pass by in its normal fashion. I settled in to the saddle more comfortably, and began to drift off, allowing my travel to become almost automated – the state in which I was snapped back to reality from shortly after. This snap came in the shape of a large roundabout I was approaching at approximately nineteen miles per hour. Initially, this was a shock; the majority of my training routes had been country lanes, and secondly because the Devon countryside has very few roundabouts - let alone ones with six or more exits! Feeling a little dazed and overwhelmed or at least inexperienced by the situation I slowed. This change in pace was enough for me to gather my thoughts. This moment of contemplation I recalled that although I may have not approached many roundabouts while on a bicycle I had, however, approached hundreds if not thousands of them while covering the hundred and seventy odd thousand miles around the British Isles in my time behind the wheel of a motor car, and the skills were transferable to the situation in question. As I came within a few metres from the junction I noticed the entrance and required exit were marked out with orange flags indicating our route and within a matter of minutes I had safely traversed the traffic and was powering along the open road feeling far more in my element as the surrounding scenery became the more familiar sight of crop fields and small country hamlets. The miles fell with a comfortable rate until I was taken by the sight of James Everson, only this time he was stopped in a layby having a rest and munching on some small snack. As I had a very comprehensive tool kit in my panniers, I enquired if he or any of the other cyclists he was sitting with had any mechanical issues to which they replied politely not as they waved me on by at a steady pace. Some twenty minutes passed before I was once again passed by James and the group he was cycling with only this time the ground was for the most part flat so I was able to match their pace and follow behind them for the next few miles until the terrain ascended the next slope. As I began to lose my pace I slipped back, allowing a sizable gap to form between myself and the group I had been following. This hill was not in any way as violent as the first, and I was soon in sight of the summit. At the summit I took a moment to review my route map I had secured to my handle bars along with the emergency contact information provided by the support team. I estimated that I was some five or six miles from the first water stop/check-in point. Setting off down the hill I set myself down in to the frame, becoming a more aerodynamic shape on the road. Now most cyclists I talk to tell me they enjoy the burn of powering up a hill but don't enjoy the feeling of acceleration afforded by gravity pulling you down the hill, due to the idea that they don't feel in complete control. On the other hand I feel far too strained keeping pace up a slope, but really feel a rush, the need for speed like a race car driver when traveling downhill. It was a short while down the road again when I met the first of the three men I would end up spending some three hundred odd miles cycling with. This man was Ajay Trione. Ajay, you see, was a man of Indian descent and was in his late thirties, and clearly someone who although suffering from the middle age spread, was basically in good shape. My first impression of Ajay was that he was from the city and held a position in middle management or some sort of other administrative vocation. This was assumed from a number of visual and verbal clues for example all his cycling gear was expensive brands but not racing kit like a lot of the die-hard cyclists on the trip; his bike was in fact the very type I would in hindsight suggest any beginner should buy if undertaking such a trip straight off the bat with only limited training. The bike in question was a Boardman Comp which due to its lightweight frame combined with a more upright seating and lower gearing made it a far easier beast to power up hills, but although not capable of the same turn of speed as my own it also possessed wider semi knobbly tyres making it more stable but slower to react to changes in surface. Generally speaking it was far wiser a choice of ride for someone of little experience partaking in events such as the L2P. Before I was able to properly engage Ajay in conversation, we rounded a bend and had caught up with Ajay's cycling partner Abrar Gill. Abrar was a man of similar ethnic and professional background as Ajay. Abrar was slightly smaller than Ajay in physical stature, but equally well equipped for the journey, sporting an almost identical outfit with a bike that was a model one rung higher up the same range as Ajay's. From the initial conversation it was clear that Abrar was the more confident and open a speaker as well as being in slightly better physical shape than either Ajay or, I suspected, myself. As conversation flowed from topic to topic I learnt that they were friends from their university days who could not spend as much time together as they may have liked to due to the responsibilities of adult life, and fairly substantial physical distance between them. In an effort to maintain their friendship as well as reclaim the physical fitness they had enjoyed during their time at university, they had decided to take up cycling, and met up to train for events that they would then enter together; events starting with 60-100 mile one day outings ramping up to events such as the L2P and doubtless beyond. Coming to the base of what looked like steep but fairly short hill reiterated that even for my youth there was no guarantee that I would be able to keep pace with my new found friends all the way to the top. This comment was met with a mute response from Ajay, and Abrar who was a few feet in front of us simply told me to do all I felt I could. As it was, the hill was no match for my fitness and I kept quiet so I could concentrate on my cadence. I was able to keep on Ajay's tail with relative ease. This fact came as a bit of a shock to both Ajay and Abrar who stopped at the top of the hill anticipating a need to regroup, and found me parked up behind them not struggling up the hill as we all first expected. As we pushed off, the road quickly levelled out and the hedge rows receded from the road side to reveal the start of a small narrow pavement which dipped in places to allow vehicle access to the occasional quaint little cottage. As the cottages became more closely packed we rounded a large sweeping bend to be greeted with the sight of a village green. This large open space was bordered by intersecting roads and loosely surrounded by the occasional large old oak tree interspaced with lines to two or three park benches. It was under one of these oak trees that we spotted a couple of trestle tables, a van, and a long flowing flag of action medical research, all surrounded by some fifty cyclists.

This was our first water stop; the first twenty-four miles of our journey had been completed. We scooted over to the table where we had to sign in to say we had arrived successfully; after giving our names we were instructed to take water and/or squash from the plastic barrels at the end of the table, help ourselves to any fruit, sweets and cereal bars from the selection available, and to rest up for a brief moment before embarking whenever we felt comfortable to set off on the next leg of forty miles taking us to our lunch stop. As I had already consumed both of my 700ml water bottles and some of my wine gums, I made sure that I refilled with these items as well as taking a banana and a tracker bar before pushing my bike over to a couple of park benches where Ajay, and Abrar were sitting resting while quietly inspecting the map. Once I had swallowed the final chunk of banana and thrown the skin in the bin which separated the two benches, I politely engaged in the conversation and enquired as to the guys' feelings on me continuing to cycle with them. To my relief this was received in a positive light and the topic was quickly directed by Abrar on to how soon the three of us felt ready to embark on the next leg, realising that people had stopped arriving and that the semi pro's and the real front runners had already left some minutes ago. With this the three of us seemed reenergised. It was then that a further revelation struck Abrar; the fact that he needed to pee. Which was unfortunately something the support crew were unable to facilitate, and could only explain that we may as well get going as we were bound to come across a public toilet somewhere soon on the route as we were about to come across slightly more densely packed population a few miles up the road. Lining up at the edge of the road one by one we three were joined by eight other cyclists who all pushed off at the same time. Glancing back for one last look before we disappeared round the next bend I could count some thirty plus cyclists still resting on the green. Our expanded group only lasted for around the first two to three miles before differentiating back to two groups of four and our threesome. As our original three cycled up a small hill, into a small town, Abrar's need for a lavatory got more and more pressing. We came to a petrol station that advertised a brand of coffee and claimed to have a mini supermarket on site, it was here that relief was found for poor Abrar who spent a good fifteen minutes inside and returned having emptied his bladder, then purchased a coffee. As soon as we had chance to set off, once again we were overtaken by another group of cyclists; this group was one of the two four packs that had departed the first water stop at the same time as us but had not at the time kept up with our chosen pace, in the same way that the three of us could not keep up with the pace set by the other group of four riders who had sprinted off ahead.

Returning to our cycling groove and picking the pace up slightly the rest of the mileage through the country roads towards the lunch stop were pleasant, but largely uneventful. Until we found ourselves at the top of very steep sloping hill that would have looked out across a wide flood plain below if it wasn't for a heavy canopy of trees overhead. I knew that we could not have been far from our lunch stop and were definitely hot on the tail of the front half of the list to check in if we could keep up the pace we had made, or better it even. With this in mind and using my natural speed demon sensibility once the bike started to accelerate with the pull of gravity, I hunkered down aerodynamically into the frame and concentrated on the road ahead of me. Due to this slight disregard for my own safety by the base of the hill I had lost Abrar and Ajay, passed several other cyclists and even overtook a small number of cars as I was hurtling a long at some 66miles per hour. Allowing the bike to return to a more comfortable speed before once again beginning to pedal it was only a few moments before all that I had passed while rocketing down the hill caught up and passed me, returning ·everything back to its natural order once again. Re-joining my cycling buddies I enquired how their legs were feeling and found that the three of us were comfortably in the zone, and felt that we could go on like this for a great many miles to come, as it was, we had travelled so far together that our lunch stop was in fact nearby as we entered a shallow forested valley, and the road ran close to a stream as it cut a zig zag path through the forest. Rounding a tight bend we were taken into a clearing where on the right hand side there was a turning in to a little level car park containing a small brick built building that looked as though it would have served as a village hall or maybe a Methodist church. By the front door there was the now familiar sight of dozens of resting cyclists and our busy support team. For the first time that day, it was starting to look cloudy overhead so parking our bikes neatly against the right hand hedge we signed in and were instructed to venture indoors where we found tables of food, mainly chicken with pasta or rice dishes, some fruit and vegetables, bowls of sweets and tracker bars, and this time two large serving trays of chocolate cake. These tables were in the middle of the hall; at one end of the hall were two large stills of hot water for tea and coffee and at the other end a small curtain shrouded stage. Looking round the room I was shocked not to find any chairs of any description, so the three of us decided that once we had suitably piled our paper plates with all manner of food available we would sit on the edge of the stage and enjoy our lunch. It was at this point that I fell in to an age old habit of mine, telling somewhat crap jokes and spouting off random facts about microbiology and genetics. This performance became to a certain extent reminiscent of my evening with Stuart at Crediton train station, although this time I decided not to push my luck as it would have made the rest of the trip uncomfortable or lonely had I allowed myself to become some highly annoying super geek. Finding a suitable point to withdraw, I made my apologies and made my way to a toilet. The toilet was small and very basic decorated with white tiles from floor to shoulder height, and then had mushroom coloured paintwork up to the ceiling. After using the facilities fully taking expert care over hand hygiene as to be expected from someone well versed in infection control and microbiological laboratory techniques, I exited the toilet and made my way out of the building. Returning to my bicycle I found Ajay and Abrar seemingly at the end of a conversation with another cyclist. This individual wasn't properly introduced to me at this point but being the calm, friendly and open person I am, the situation did not feel strained, the unknown individual was later in the day introduced to me as Harshal Kshatri, a man roughly one year older than myself, from West Croydon but with Indian ancestry. He was someone who will later an play important role in the events to come on my trip to Paris, but at the time in question he was no more than another cyclist and so the conversation went no more in-depth than to discuss the pros and cons of different bicycles when undertaking a challenge such as we were taking part in. Being in a much more refuelled and ready a state, Harshal left the conversation and quickly returned to his bike to set off on the afternoon leg of the day's route. This departure left the remaining three of Ajay, Abrar and me discussing our first impressions of our new acquaintance, one resounding point that the three of us all picked up on was the amount of times he had mentioned his shop during the conversation without actually divulging any actual description of the shop, its location, stock, staff, or business type. Our topic of conversation quickly changed back to a more cycle related matter once we realised that our insight in to the man that is Harshal Kshatri had left more questions than it had answered. Our new talking point was chamois butter, which I was at the time liberally reapplying to the inside of my legs, while discreetly hiding from view between one of the support vans and a nearby hedge. Once my cycling outfit was comfortably repositioned and I was equally repositioned on my wheels the three of us again set off on the afternoon's cycle.

The ride commenced in much the same way as it had the rest of the day, and that is how I expected it to stay, but sadly I was very much incorrect, half way between the lunch stop and next water stop the first of what would eventually become many minor disasters fell upon me. Allow me to set the scene. The three of us had come to a road bridge over a busy duel carriageway. Set in to the road surface on either side of the bridge was a border of narrow slatted metal structures that resembled cattle grids. Now, being a relatively heavy lad riding on a bike with some of the narrowest tyres available - a rigid aluminium frame with a tiny saddle - this gave me an issue. My issue was because of this, the first of these grids, gave me a pair of short sharp painful shocks to my gluteus maximus, making my next few moments of riding very uncomfortable, then just as my body began to return to normal, with the front tyre and road contacting rubber, I hit the second of these grids. Once again this sent a mind rousingly painful shock though me. My body prepared itself for the rear wheel to connect with the cause of my discomfort only this time it was accompanied by a loud pop from underneath my slightly bruised posterior. This signified the first puncture, bringing my progress to a halt, with the guys already powering up the next hill, and so out of earshot. Now due to a bad bit of packing on my part, although I had a full complement of tools in my day luggage I found out that my spare inner tube supply was in my overnight luggage, which was in the back of the support van ending for our overnight stop over. With this knowledge my only option was to lift the bike aloft, strap it across my broad shoulders and furiously sprint up the slope until I nearly collapsed into a hedge. Swaying wildly from left to right, trying to remain upright, I carefully took the bike from off my shoulders and stood it back on the ground next to me, grasping the saddle post. Realising that I had made quite a significant distance up the hill from the scene of the accident I felt compelled to continue on. I leaned forward, now placing one hand on the centre of the bike's handle bars while lifting the back end of the bike up by the saddle post so the rear wheel lost contact with the road, allowing me to scoot the bike along in a sort of wheelbarrow-like fashion. Within a minute I rounded the next bend to find Abrar and Ajay chilling out in the shade of what looked like a miniature chapel constructed of wood walls with concrete blocks as foundations, with a little red brick paved area on the ground in front. They had noticed my disappearance and had stopped for a few moments to allow me time to catch up. Once I had briefly explained my predicament, Abrar kindly offered me one of his supply of inner tubes and we set about getting my bike back to full functionality. A process that took seconds rather than minutes but did leave Abrar looking slightly shocked as he read the tyre pressure on the wall of my rear tyre; as it was, my tyres wanted to be pumped to one hundred pounds per square inch. Without access to a proper track pump eighty psi was the best we could achieve. Once sitting back on the bike I couldn't really feel much difference between the front and rear and the bike reacted to the terrain almost identically to how it had done before the incident, so we were soon back up to speed and pushing hard to make up for the minor delay we had encountered. It seemed to take ages although it was in actual fact only some fifteen minutes, until we had found ourselves back in the realms of civilization. Amongst lots of relatively new built houses and homes, at the end of the road was large open park, with an intermittently tree lined perimeter off in the distance and a low rising brick wall marking out the near boundary, and a van was parked on the grass under a great oak tree a little distance from the wall. As we approached we saw that this was in fact one of our support vehicles and that this was our third and final water stop of our first day cycling. As we pulled up and signed in on the register, it was clear that we were not long behind the majority of the other riders and were still in front of a couple of the really slow groups. This news was frustrating to a minor degree, as it meant we could possibly catch up with some more of the other riders if we set off quickly and kept up a quick pace. Feeling energised by the challenge we made light work of our explanation for our delay thus far. On hearing the tale of my tyre and that the replacement inner tube was only inflated to 80% of the recommended pressure it was recommended by the support team that they should pressurise the tyre using the standing track pump to get me moving in best form to catch up. With my road-going rubber back to full strength I remounted my ride and the three of us prepared to set off. To my horror within the first rotation of my wheels my rear tyre blew a second inner tube, once again halting my progress and making me feel like even more of a disappointing hindrance to my cycling partners. Dredging the bottom of my pit of sorrow I was feeling an all-encompassing rage of self-hatred and crushing self-doubt, when one of the women from the support team informed me that one of the charity's staff riders had come down with something, preventing them from completing that day's ride. The offer was made for me to temporarily swap bikes while she rode the rest of the day in one of the support vans to concentrate on her recuperation. Lifting my unfortunate bicycle into the back of the van, I was told not to despair and that once we had arrived at our overnight stop in Calais one of the mechanics from the main support van would be able to get my little white friend back on the road properly.

Stepping over the frame and mounting my borrowed wheels, I thanked the support crew for lending me the bicycle and signalled to Abrar and Ajay to set off as they were slightly downhill. I knew it wouldn't take long for my excessive downhill speed to make up the distance. Settling down in to the saddle I cautiously got moving. Picking up speed I began to notice the difference between my little white chariot and the metallic grey/blue one I had been loaned. Designed for a woman, the saddle was wider with deeper, softer padding which was like an armchair compared to the hard, aerodynamic, arse-shattering one on my own bike. Although it was far more comfortable to sit on it was like fighting with a straitjacket trying to get my legs in a position that I could put power down on the pedals. Equally frustrating was the difference in the frame shape which lent itself to a more comfortable but less aerodynamic upright riding position compared to the hunkered down streamlined position I was used to riding in. The gear change was in an easier to access position than mine but its operation was far more tasking due it having an extra 60% more gears to choose from. These small issues were easy to overlook as I was just happy to be back on the road rocking along as part of the ride's most ethnically diverse cycling team on our route to Paris. The conversation between the three of us was quite muted and I did not engage with the guys quite as fluidly as I had earlier in the day. This was mainly due to my lingering self-disappointment and anger. After a short spell on a fast country road we forked off to the left up a much smaller road, which took us up a hill past a very small wooded landscape. As the summit of the hill the horizon fell away to reveal a wide bottomed valley that looked to be a dried up river bed with once associated flood plains. Cutting discreetly along the valley floor, following what I imagined was the path of the long forgotten river was a wide gravel track, loosely tarmacked in sections. Once we had taken a quick moment to take in the wonderful sight of our surroundings we made our way down the hill side to the gravel track and began to make our way along the base of the valley. Being on the loaned bike I felt far more comfortable on the loose ground than I imagined I would have felt on the skinny tyres of my own. Within a few minutes we heard the sounds of a larger road a little way ahead; cycling on for a few more minutes the valley sides fell away to a large open plain and the sight of the road we had heard. It was cutting right across the landscape in front of us. As we rounded the last bend of the gravel track in the style of high performance rear wheel drive drift race track day cars, our rear tyres spat clouds of dust and gravel high into the air behind us. We approached the mouth where the gravel track met the road and noticed another of our orange route marking flags instructing us to turn left on to the smooth tarmac in front of us. It wasn't long till we again found ourselves back on small country lanes bordered with thick tall green hedges. These continued seemingly unbroken for mile after mile. That was until the three of us came across a building that looked like a perfect example of any old English postcard scene, a Tudor built large country cottage set in its own picturesque garden of rose bushes by the junction of two quiet country lanes. Due to the size of the building my mind was rolling trying to decide its most probable function that it once served, which I settled as being a small pub or tearoom. As we approached yet another orange flag was spied instructed us to turn right down the road next to the beautiful house. As we did I took the opportunity to take a longer look at the gardens which strengthen my belief that the place was a tearoom due to the back garden having a number of small tables. It was here however that the three of us came close to literally bumping into another group of cyclists from our route. We stopped but did not fully dismount as we asked if they were having an issue to which they replied they were unsure and were debating what route to take. This perplexed me a little as I had felt the route was obvious as I had already seen an orange flag off in the distance down the straight road we had just turned on to, but had luckily completely missed what looked on close inspection to be faded and damaged or a badly produced replica to my left instructing the unfortunate to turn down a narrow and rather muddy lane on my right. It was clear from tyre tracks both options had been taken recently by more than one individual which increased the confusion. The seven of us decided the best option was to phone the rear support van to see if they were close and could advise. Before any of us had successfully reached for our phones, another couple of cyclists turned up followed closely by the support van, who confirmed my suspicions that the off colour orange flag to my left had been tampered with and was not supposed to be pointing down the muddy road and had probably been played with by some anarchistic little scrotum of an individual. With this knowledge we all mounted our wheels and the nine of us set off together knowing we were running incredibly short on time to get to the meeting point in Dover. Back on the road and pushing hard I was once again lost in the splendour of the day and the lovely quiet middle England scenery for miles; we cycled on, passing road signs that slowly counted down the distance to our destination. We came to a large steep hill which seemed to carry on for ages. The longer we travelled up the hill the slower and slower we began to travel. As our rate of travel became no more than a slow jogging pace we snaked left to right across the road trying to as hard as we could to keep the pedals turning in a regular fluid motion. A few yards further the gradient became yet steeper, it was at this point that collectively our legs couldn't take any more of the stress; almost simultaneously we all dismounted and reached for our water bottles. Once the fire in our legs had died slightly, we decided we would push the bikes up the hill having no clue how long it would go on for; being the youngest I took point and jogged on as fast as my worn legs would allow, scooting my bike along beside me. Turning the corner a few metres up the road I was shocked to find that we had in fact broken the back of it as the gradient almost instantly fell away to a gentle slope up to the crest of the hill some hundred metres ahead. This relief was enough to energise our group to jump back on our frames and peddle like fury all the way to the top where the lane met a main road which we were to turn right on to and follow at speed as it cut across the landscape down in to the outskirts of Dover. As we did so we noticed our orange arrows started to be joined by similarly sized yellow ones pointing in the corresponding directions. This was a welcome sight as we had been told during the briefing that morning that this was to signify the convergence of our route with another similar route being taken by an almost identical group of riders from a different charity, which would be catching the same ferry. As the scenery became progressively more urbanised, the roads became busier and we found our speed being dictated by the flow of traffic instead of the amount of physical punishment our bodies could cope with. Passing several streets of little houses we came around a corner to the sight of a small pub on the opposite side of the road. Packed in to the small beer garden in front were a small number of bicycles and sitting in the early evening sun were their riders, some of whom I recognised as being part of our route. This was due to the fact they had made such good time getting to Dover that they had arrived with time to stop and enjoy a cold beverage before making the final mile trundle to the meeting point. We didn't stop to chat, only giving a wave and a polite hello as we rolled past at a very relaxed pace. Minutes later we arrived at the designated car park to be greeted by the sight of the majority of the other riders from our party all congregating round one of the pay and display parking ticket machines. Dismounting our rides and joining the congregation, there was a faint air of triumph about as everybody was congratulating each other on the mileage we had all covered, swapping stories of sights and incidents seen, the seasoned veterans explaining that the day was not over although the next stage of proceedings was by far the easiest so far. More cyclists arrived and so the chatter became progressively louder until our support van arrived to take the register to make sure we had all made it on time. It was at this point I had the chance to properly meet the woman whose bike I had been riding albeit very briefly as we were soon being marshalled back out of the car park down the road and around the corner to the ferry terminal. The ferry terminal building looked a large hut with a small coach park in front and a large blue and white sign standing high above the roof displaying the words 'Port of Dover'. Being the first major landmark of the journey this prompted several cyclists to reveal cameras they had concealed about their cycling gear and begin creating the first evidence of our trip. This however did not go without out its own comedy moment. Due to the size and height of the building, the sign and the compact nature of the coach park people found it difficult to get a shot of their cycling buddies without chopping out the edges of the sign or obscuring certain letters leading to many of the photos being at places such as, the 'ort of Dover', 'Port of over', or my personal favourite the 'Pot of Dove'. During this photographic mayhem I began to talk with a couple of riders I had not had chance to introduce myself to earlier in the day, and enquire why it was that they were far more muddy than the rest of us. The reason for this was that they were the individuals who had been sent down the muddy lane by the interfered-with arrow by the tearoom a few miles outside of Dover. A call sounded from the support crew that it was time for us to make our way out of the coach park up the slipway to the left of the building where we were instructed to queue in pairs so we could push our bikes along as we were marshalled slowly on to the ferry. As we did so the atmosphere became damp. It was very grey overhead and it was hard to tell exactly what was actually rain falling, and what was sea spray, as we edged up the ramp in to the vehicle deck. We were informed that we needed to stay to the left and to continue forward as far as possible to the front of the ship to help the flow of vehicles boarding and maintain prompt departure. We neatly rested our bikes against the side walls to the front of the ship and used bike locks to secure them in place as the rest of the ferry filled with lorries, cars campervans and caravans. Once we were given the all clear we made our way to the stair wells in the centre of the ship to take us up to the passenger lounges. Once reunited as a foursome, Abrar, Ajay, Harshal and I found a table at the front of the ship with a large window from where we could watch our exit from English shores. It was at this point I realised the time was about half past six and that in my little corner of England my family would be sitting down to dinner. As the ferry began to move, I left the table and made my way to the rear of the ship to make a call home. My phone had reception and half the battery left but as I couldn't guarantee how long either of those would last for I quickly dialled my home number. The answer was timely, after a couple of rings my mother picked up - they had all just finished eating. My mother was, as I expect most would be, quick to ask if I was OK. Once I had answered her worries and relayed the highlights and lowlights of my day the phone was passed to my father with whom I had a near identical conversation before it was passed finally to Rosie. Our conversation was as factual to begin with but quickly turned in to a series of back and forth 'I love yous' interspaced with periods of random noise such as hmm and ohm, whispered in an affectionate manner, that was until my phone beeped to exclaim its battery was running low. We decided it was best left at that, said our goodbyes and Rosie wished me luck for my coming few days' travel before we hung up. Returning to our table at the front of the ferry I re-joined the conversation. The discussion revolved around the fact that Harshal was a shop keeper. Although it was not clear what type of establishment it was as Harshal seemed to be in the business of all sorts of different sectors of retail, selling an intriguing combination of items he wanted to be in the market for and the items that the local populous required of him. This was something I sympathised with; after my working day was over I often spent time talking business plans with my mother who was the proprietor of a small jewellery shop in Ilfracombe high street. Although our business and natural habitats were very different I found that Harshal and I had a great deal in common, at this point I picked up on Harshal's trance word. For anyone not clued up on this little piece of popular social psychology, a 'trance word' is a word, phrase, or statement often repeated by an individual or select group, these words get slipped in to conversation subconsciously regardless of their relevance to the rest of the dialogue. This occurs as a sort of subconscious comfort mechanism for the individual to gauge the safety of their place within the group. Picking up on people's trance words and using them yourself when speaking with that person or group will enhance the rapport and the chemistry build up between you. As with most people I have no clue off the top of my head what my own trance words would be but I have no doubt that were you to talk to me in the presence of my close friends and family they would become apparent very quickly. Returning to the moment in question, for Harshal his quickly obvious trance words were 'my shop' which featured in nearly every sentence he said. Even when questioned about cycling the answer still involved reference to his business. Now it has to be said often there was good reasoning for this. For example, the bike that Harshal was using to take him to Paris had come to him from a business contact of his. Very quickly I found myself interjecting my opinion on whatever the current topic was, preceded with 'at my shop' in reference to my mother's jewellery shop. This would also set a precedent for how the majority of our conversations went over the coming days.

The next topic of conversation was the accommodation arrangements for the coming evening. This was something I had not really given much thought to that point. The reason for my lack of forward thinking was the knowledge that the responsibility for the arrangements had been that of the charity's well experienced team. That, coupled with the fact that I am an avid festival goer and camper had no issues with sleeping rough should we had been required to. At this point Ajay explained that he and Abrar had found their accommodation information earlier in the day and already knew that for them at least there was not a tent in sight. They knew they were staying the night in a twin room in a budget

Calais hotel. They had brought up the topic to say they were mildly interested if Harshal or I, or both of us had been put in the same hotel. Now, the card with my information was attached to my bike some two levels below and so I was not able to do as Harshal did and produce it from a pocket to begin reading it. A few minutes passed till Harshal placed the card back in his pocket, turned to the three of us and announced that he was staying at a different hotel to Ajay and Abrar; he was staying at a hotel which sounded to be of a higher status. He continued by saying that he had been allocated a shared room with a Mr N R Elwell, at which point I exclaimed "Dude, that's me!" which was met with an air of relief as now we all knew where we were going to be resting, and that we were at least on good speaking terms with the person on the other side of the room.

The conversation paused for a while as we looked out of the windows at the sight of our destination harbour; we had not realised but we had in fact arrived in France and seconds later we heard the call for us to return to our bikes. As we made our way to the stairs we met with all the other cyclists we had met during the day who were followed by all the van and car drivers slowly returning to their vehicles. The stairwells were very crowded until the doors to the car deck below were opened and we were all allowed sight of our respective metal. Back in the car deck, for my three cycling partners and me at least, our bikes were exactly as we had left them - chained to each other with the cheapest being the most visible. Together they were equally well secured to the side of the ship. As the large vehicles around us started to disembark, the rest of our hundred plus cycling force readied itself to do the same. We were instructed that once back on terra firma we would find one of our support vans parked to the left a few metres clear of the ramp, and that we were to congregate behind it and await further instruction. This came in the form of one of our mechanics hanging one handed from the folded rear door of the van, as he called to us down a megaphone. He explained how we were to exit the port and cycle in to Calais itself where we would find our hotels; he also informed us that our rooms and keys had already been allocated to us and that at each hotel we would find a representative of our support team who would supply us with our room keys as well as direct us to our rooms, via the bike storage facility. Also they would be able to reunite us with our luggage which had arrived at our overnight destinations earlier that afternoon. Moments later we were back on our bikes scooting along in a long snaking line of pairs behind the van. As we approached the customs' check points to my left I noticed we were close to the boundary fence, a thick wire mesh standing some twelve feet tall. On the other side of the fence was a road which the cyclists who had been at the front of the queue were now cycling along. As we passed through the gates out of the port itself and turned down the road to head in to the town I felt a strange internal turmoil. On one hand pride with what had so far been accomplished and on the other disappointment that I was not only one of the youngest riders there but depressingly also among the slowest ten to fifteen percent. This was compounded by the realisation that I was getting very hungry. Snapping back in to focus I began to trundle down the road at a comfortable pace keeping one eye down on the road below me due to a network of tram lines which would have spelled disaster if one of my wheels fell in to one awkwardly. As we came in to the centre of the town we were instructed to turn left on to a wide well-lit street; we had been told that the hotel Harshal and I would be staying in would be found first and that Abrar and Ajay's was the final port of call. But in my hunger I completely missed this and continued to cycle along taking note of the bars and stereotypical Parisian styled French cafes with their large open gazebo-like street level outside dining spaces, and totally missed mine and Harshal's hotel, cycling straight past the main entrance without even noticing the rep standing on the pavement outside. Blindly we cycled on in to an even wider space marked out by ranks of closed shops and white tiled pavements filled with market stalls in the centre some sort of a long rectangular traffic island, again covered in yellow and off white titles, with vehicles parked around it and some form of one way system splitting the flow of traffic to travel down opposite sides of the island dependent on direction of travel. Cycling along through this area we found the surfaces very slippy which made the bike feel a little unsteady. These feelings were compounded by the sight of a number of other cyclists coming off their bikes as their tyre grip gave way on the slippery surface. Carefully leaving this area we returned to more normal roads until we came across a member of the support crew who was flagging us to turn down the road to our right slowing down to allow us to have a short conversation; we found that this was the way Ajay and Abrar needed to go to get to their hotel and that Harshal and I needed to turn around and travel back through the town as our hotel was quite a way back up the way we had just come from, back on the other side of the while tiled area. Upon being informed that we had in fact travelled an unnecessary additional mile and would now have to do so again to get where we were meant to be, Harshal and I immediately turned one hundred and eighty degrees, said good night to our cycling partners and sped off in search of our beds. As we cycled back along the roads we had just come down we passed several cyclists looking for the same hotel as Abrar and Ajay and so were able to inform them that they were heading in the correct direction and didn't have much farther to go. Returning to the white tiled area we once again witnessed several riders fighting to keep their bikes upright and stop them from sliding out from underneath their legs. A few had been smart enough to have hopped off and started walking the bike along. Minutes later we were in sight of the road of restaurants I had noted earlier when I noticed directly across the road from one was a large building with large glass sliding doors and a sign above saying Mercure Metro. It was then that I noticed the woman with a clip board standing on the pavement outside frantically waving and signalling to us.

We had finally made it. Pulling up to the entrance we were instructed to turn around and take the first alley on the left round to the rear of the hotel to find the bike storage. Doing so we found a little loading bay, like a factory goods in department, with a concrete ramp to one of the rear doors of the building. Dismounting and pushing our bikes up the ramp in single file, I was happy when the door opened to reveal the woman whom we had spoken to out the front, and a room full of bikes. We signed in and listened to a brief explanation of the plan for the following morning before being given our keys and directed to our room. On the third floor of the building our room was a comfortable size with a large open plan clothes rail behind the door, a television in the middle of that wall, and directly opposite the footboards of a pair of standard single beds, which were positioned two feet from and in parallel with the side walls and three or four feet apart from each other in the middle. Each bed was allocated a bed side light plug socket on top of an individual chest of drawers. Sitting on a bed each we browsed the TV's channels till we found one with English news. Due to the hour and rumble of our empty stomachs we decided that once our luggage was delivered to our room we would have a shower each and get a fresh change of clothes on then head out to find some food as it felt too early to hit the sack for the night. Within minutes there was a commanding knock at the door signifying the arrival of our luggage. At this point I started rummaging through my suitcase to find my wash bag. Taking it in turns we used the en suite bathroom. The bathroom was a sensible size, pale grey lino floor, white tiles from the floor to approximately waist height and magnolia paint up to and including the ceiling. At one end was a glass panelled shower with a rack of towels next to it. At the other end of the room by a little half frosted window was the toilet which was across from the bathroom door. Next to the door was a sink with a well-lit vanity mirror. Now I must at this point digress into explaining a slightly sort of taboo subject. Therefore as a warning to anyone reading this who has a slightly timid or easily shocked nature you have been warned, continue reading the next paragraph at your own risk; you have been dutifully cautioned.

If there are any girlfriends, wives, or partners of any form reading this who wish to get their partner to shower more regularly or for whatever reason wish to spend more time in the shower, take note of this next piece of information. Changing their shower gel for one with mint and/or tea tree could be the answer. A number of years before, I had quite innocently bought some shower gel containing mint and tea tree and had accidentally discovered the incredible sensations that can come from their use on the male or for that matter female private parts. These sensations can only be described as very gentle electric shocks starting at the genitals and spreading out to the rest of the body. This sensation has made for some interesting shower experiences over the past couple of decades of my life. These shower gels can also add an addition level of fun to a sexual and intimate shower shared between lovers.

Returning to our story so far; I stepped out from the shower and dried my body off and proceeded to apply liberal amounts of tiger balm to the inside of my thighs before wrapping myself in a large towel so I could step out of the bathroom into the main room where Harshal was sitting at the end of his bed watching the world outside through the window. Returning to my side of the room I said to Harshal that the bathroom was free. Once I was alone I began to get dressed. Dropping my towel and slipping in to a fresh pair of boxer short underwear followed by a soft pair of grey cotton trousers and a paisley shirt, then sitting at the end of my bed, I waited for Harshal to return. Moments later he emerged from the bathroom wrapped in a towel. To give the guy the same respect as he had shown me I returned to the bathroom to brush my teeth leaving him to the privacy of the room to get dressed. I also used this time to splash myself with a little of my Davidoff *Cool Water* eau de toilette. Once again returning to the room we were almost ready to hit the outside world. I took my phone off of its charger and grabbed my wallet and our key card. Once I had slipped in to a pair of extremely bright multi coloured animal flip flops we proceeded to the stairs. Back on the ground floor we made our way round to the reception area at the entrance of the hotel. As we passed the desk we said good evening to the woman working on reception, the entrance lobby of the hotel consisted of a long narrow corridor of large panel mirrors with a glass door at each end. The door in front of the reception desk was a metal framed single panel of plain glass. The door at the other end which led out on the street outside, this was a wide revolving affair we had to negotiate to make our way out to the road outside. Out on the road side I felt a mix of feelings including pride for having accomplished the first day of our journey, and a feeling of gratitude for how well I had gotten on with Harshal, Abrar, Ajay and the other riders, knowing that had it not been for them the trip so far might not have been such a pleasant one. This happy state was mildly tainted with feelings of sorrow and selfishness that I wasn't directly sharing the experience with my family and Rosie. Most of all I was feeling in desperate need of food, leading to regret that I didn't eat something on the ferry or back in Dover. It was clear from his face Harshal was going through a similar thought process. The air was crisp and as the last of the day's sunlight ebbed away we wandered up and down the road trying to decide on where we were going to eat. The restaurant directly across the road from our hotel looked nice and comfortable with its heated gazebo dining area out on the pavement, its menu also looked somewhat expensive in a much faked Parisian style, it mimicked very closely one of the restaurants Rosie and I had opted to dine in during our previous romantic weekend in Paris some six months before. Now due to the fact that neither Harshal nor I had any real mastery of the French language and were both mindful of our budgets having to last the rest of the trip, we decided to give the place a miss in preference for an English seaside styled fish and chip shop Harshal had noticed on the corner at the far end of the street. Walking up to it the place was small and quite greasy looking with two sets of metal tables and chairs outside on the pavement, this time not surrounded by a gazebo differentiating them from the rest of the pavement, just placed either side of the door under the neon light of the white faced shop sign above. The menu was simple, written in bold text in both French and English. Upon entering it was clear the proprietor was well versed in dealing with English tourists, his command of my mother tongue was far greater than mine of his. Feeling no pressure to do so, Harshal and I decided that we would still make a somewhat butchered attempt each to ask in French for a portion of chips with cheese. Harshal in fact went one better asking for curry sauce as well. Turning to me the guy behind the counter inquired wisely in English if I wanted curry sauce as well. To which I answered yes. Moments later we were sitting on the slightly cold metal chairs outside in the cool late evening air enjoying our chips and talking about any random topics that came to mind. For a good forty minutes we sat and in that time, I rambled on about everything dear to me. My family, girlfriend, guitars, microbiology and genetics, cars, friends and rugby team mates. Harshal was receptive to it all and in return educated me in aspects of his life such as his now legendary shop and his involvement in his local football team. Once we realised our chips had been finished for some time now we decided to take a small walk around the block to help with their digestion before returning to our hotel. This procedure for returning to our room was basically the reverse of how we had left the building, first negotiating the revolving door and the corridor of mirrors before saying good night to the night staff, only this time we opted to find our floor using the lift rather than the stairs.

Back in our room I put my phone on charge next to my bed and then we again took it in turns to use the bathroom to brush our teeth, use the loo, and get dressed in our night clothes. We arranged our things ready for the morning and while exchanging pleasantries climbed in to our respective beds where we watched TV and using the hotels Wi-Fi, checked our emails and Facebook accounts for a short time before concluding we were up to date with events of the day and that it was time we started turning the lights out and attempt to get some sleep. Now anyone who has ever had to share a room with me will tell you once I have fallen asleep I don't move. I have an almost magical ability; I often wake in the exact same position I last was in before nodding off.

Chapter Nineteen
Day Two: Calais to Arras

The morning that followed the evening in Calais was a gentle but early one, after once again taking turns in the bathroom to shower, brush teeth and finally use the loo. We set about getting dressed in our cycling gear. This included liberal use of my chamois butter on my legs while squeezing myself in to a clean pair of my tight cycling shorts. Donning a fresh bright yellow cycling top I felt excited about the challenges we would face on our second day on the road to Paris. Once Harshal and I were fully packed up, we made our way downstairs to the breakfast room. Stepping into the breakfast room I saw a sea of the familiar faces of all the other cyclists who had stayed at the hotel that night. I spied a free table close to a window and next to the table of a rather muscle bound Kiwi fella. Sitting down at the table briefly I looked at the world outside, the sun was just coming up and street that we had walked along the night before was now bathed in a strange pale grey light. Rising to my feet I made my way to the breakfast buffet table to select what I fancied from the typically well-presented continental offerings. Starting as I believe an Englishman should always do with a warm, unsugared, cup of tea before moving on to choose a couple of croissants with apricot jam followed by a pain au chocolate with Nutella. Sitting back down to devour my selection I found myself shocked by the fact that I didn't feel cheated by the lack of grilled sausages, bacon and fried eggs that I usually demanded by the absolute truck load when waking up in a hotel. Finishing my food in a timely manner my mind flipped back to cycling and at this point I realised I had no idea of the state of play with my bike and if there was actually going to be a set of wheels that I could use to continue cycling with my friends at all. My next port of call was in fact to speak to one of the mechanics who informed me that my bike was back to being functional and I was able to use it for the day's journey ahead. He also explained that the reason it had managed to go through both inner tubes the day before was due to no fault of mine and nothing to do with my weight or level of fitness, it was in fact caused by the use of substandard equipment during the bike's assembly which again I had played no part in. the problem stemmed from the wheel itself. Not the rim, but inside of the rim there is band of material known as the rim tape. This is placed there to stop the tips of the spokes from coming in contact with and potentially piercing the inner tube. What he believed had happened was that the rim tape running round the inside of my wheels was not able to cope with the pressures that my tyres were recommended to be pumped up to and so was a failure waiting to happen. He also explained that he did not have the resources to completely change the whole of the rim tape; he had been only been able to patch the worst worn sections and he hoped that that would last the rest of the trip which was hopeful but given the fact that the wheels had already done seven hundred miles before the first puncture occurred there was a good chance they could survive the couple of hundred left to get me to the finish line. I didn't care what could happen down the road, I was just overjoyed to be back on my own wheels.

A short time later I had checked out, handing my room key back and had also handed my overnight luggage back to the support crew. Hauling my bike and panniers outside I met up with Harshal and couple of the other cyclists. We set off all together and soon we were passing the white tiled area we had travelled through the evening before, followed by passing the road that led down to Abrar and Ajay's hotel. I noticed other groups of our cycling fellows both in front and behind but I couldn't see if any of them were Abrar or Ajay.

As Calais fell away to rural France we joined a road which headed in a south easterly direction, passing a number of farms and small farming communities that seem to have been founded near streams or rivers that now made up a cannel like network of small managed and bridged waterways. The road ran alongside open fields that also bordered the canal. The road itself was quite wide and relatively smooth compared to the equivalent road in English farming countryside in counties such as Devon and Somerset. To my right there was a dusty and dirty narrow strip of land that ran along the road and separated it from a series of tall hedgerows which seemed to lead to slightly more wild and moorlike terrain beyond. The light was steadily becoming less grey, and the world more bright, colourful and vibrant with every passing minute, and as we rolled on, each finding our own comfortable speed, the group that had left Calais together slowly became more and more fragmented until I realised that I was cycling on my own, having not kept pace with the more semi-professional riders I had left with that morning but also having not yet been met by riders of a similar level of fitness to me. I did not have much time to contemplate the meaning of this fact before I caught sight of a familiar helmet. With his bike resting against the roadside hedge, James Everson was kneeling down on the dusty ground by the roadside up ahead of me with his camera in hand, taking photos and videos of all the cyclists who passed him. I was shortly going to be next being snapped. Wanting to look my best, chest puffed, stomach sucked in, as I drew up into his camera shot I slowed down to be able to exchange a passing comment before putting foot to pedal and accelerating off in to the morning light. Although our conversation was only a brief exchange of a couple of statements it left me feeling inspired with a thirst for the challenges that lay ahead and renewed optimism and confidence in my ability to complete the journey to Paris, enjoying the sights and friendships I was building along the way. It also reminded me that it was James' words the morning of the previous day that had inspired me to mount the challenge of the first hill we came to that day in the way I had.

Snapping back to task of keeping my wheels turning, I confidently ploughed on through the French countryside; slowly the roads became less of wide country lanes and more British main road like, and still I surged on ever closer to our first water stop of the day. We had been told that morning that the water stop for the morning was some twenty miles down the road just past a little village by the name of Ardes. Turning out on to a large seemingly fast moving road I saw sign posts for Ardes and felt that I must have been getting close which I felt was a good excuse to pause for a moment and have a large gulp of one of my water bottles patiently waiting in their frame mounted holders a few inches below me. Realising moments later that I had in fact completely drained the whole six hundred millilitre bottle in basically one sitting, it was probably high time I got back to the cycling and so set off, pushing hard to accelerate back to a quick but maintainable speed. It has to be said that the mild but bright atmospheric conditions, the smooth and relatively flat road surface and the polite French drivers who are more respectful and appreciative of cyclists than the majority of the British public all made for basically near perfect cycling conditions for me to just get down deep in the frame and pump my legs as hard as I felt was possible for a man of only mediocre cardiovascular fitness. It wasn't long before I hit the edge of

Ardes which was tiny and was somewhat reminiscent of a small Devon village near my home called Berrynarbor only a far flatter sort of French variety, built up around the intersection of a couple of country roads. It was little more than a collection of houses with no sign of any shops as I whistled through on my little white chariot, trying desperately not to disturb the peace and tranquillity of the place. A little further on down the road I spied another orange route-marking triangle. Cycling up to it I could see that it was clearly instructing me to turn off of the smooth main road on to a very wide but bumpy gravel track that stretched on into the horizon, cutting through the landscape between miles of crop fields. Pushing on down the track I felt that I could only be a couple of miles away from the water stop which was a nice thought as my bike was now out of its comfort zone on the rough stony ground, which made the ride uncomfortable and much more like hard work causing me to stop for a moment's pause with regularity; despite this annoyance I trudged on slow and steady.

Shock horror, my rhythm was broken by the now depressingly familiar pop and hiss of my rear tire, once again destroying its own inner tube, then slopping on the ground, limp and lifeless, hanging from my wheel rim like a used condom. Hopping off the bike I stood there and stared at my broken equipment for a couple of moments before I heard the sound of approaching cyclists. Over the next few minutes several small groups and couples cycled past me, each slowing down to ask if I was OK and if I required anything, or just to tell me that one of the support vans was not very far away and neither was the first water stop. In each case, I casually waved each person on as they cycled by. As I did so I used the time to take in the beauty of my surroundings in great detail; the large dark green hedgerow that run along the length of the lane to the left of me. Looking down I realised the track below me was actually quite rough and unfinished tarmac, covered with a loose scattering of stones with no regularity to their size, shape or geographic distribution. To my right there was a sheer drop off at the edge of the surface of the track down a steep but shallow turf embankment that led in to the cereal crop field which ran along the side of the track. Returning my focus back to the bike I picked the accommodation card off of the handle bar so that I could access the emergency contact information printed on the reverse. I made a call to the mechanic listed and explained my situation and rough position along the route. The advice given was to stay put and that assistance would be along shortly as they were only a few minutes back up the road. True to that a mere moment later upon the horizon I spied the sight of a van turning off the main road on to the gravel track towards me. Another short while spent with the mechanic tinkering with my ride and I was once again set to get moving. Tentatively I pulled away, keeping a highly critical and obsessively paranoid eye on the ground barely inches in front of my wheels; slowly I gathered pace but still felt the need to concentrate on the ground directly in front of me. I continued on in this manner for a short while until I rounded a corner and found I was gaining ground on the last group that passed me earlier. As I began to get within communication distance of the cyclists in front, the sight of a rather militaryesque, wide single bar, red and white metal gate could be seen partially blocking the path a little further down the road. Once past the metal gate I found that I had arrived at the site of the morning's water stop. Slowing to a crawling pace I surveyed the area. It was a wide clearing by the roadside in the middle of a small wood. Due to its geographical position far from any real high volume routes it was a secluded little spot of such gentle beauty and nature that I imagined it was surely the meeting point of local lovers and young sweethearts. The largely romantic part of my soul couldn't help but imagine what the clearing would look like to walk through at night hand in hand with my lady. Returning from my dream state to the reality of my two wheeled transport I found myself approaching a gazebo sheltered trestle table by a van. This was covered in the now standard array of tracker bars, fruit baskets, bowls of confectionery and barrels of squash. Once I had signed in, taken on some fruit, a tracker bar and refilled my water bottles, I joined all the other cyclists who were sitting in their various groups, soaking up the sun and resting gently on the grass. Finding my usual three cycling companions I explained my morning's troubles and reassured them that given just couple of minutes to rest and prepare myself mentally I would quickly be recovered and ready to hit the road again allowing the four of us to depart together without the necessity for them to be standing around for a long period just waiting to for me. Soon enough we were back on the road and the conversation had returned to the level of the previous day although one of the first topics for discussion was in fact the events of the evening before and difference in the standard of accommodation. It turned out that Harshal and I had spent the night in a far more superior class of establishment in comparison to the budget venue Ajay and Abrar had been supplied with for the evening; upon inspection of my accommodation card it was apparent that the evening ahead of us was in fact going to be the complete 180 degree turn around with Harshal and I being booked in to the budget room and Abrar and Ajay comfortably resting the night in a hotel of the same brand as we had stayed at the night before.

A little before midday the sun beat down between the occasional patch of fluffy white clouds. As it did we cycled on gently, enjoying the pretty French countryside all the while. As we came over a small hump in the landscape we saw a wonderful vista before us, a wide open grassland basin dotted with trees and wild bushes. The roadhead snaked through the land, smooth and black and disappeared from view round a large sweeping bend where the horizon met some small hills far off in the distance. As we began our descent down the road from our vantage point we periodically caught sight of the other cycling teams in front of us as they sequentially disappeared and reappeared with the periodic curvature and dipping and straightening of the road ahead. As the miles cracked on I found myself in a state of absolute harmony and tranquillity, happily cycling along feeling amazingly content with my simple life of equally simple pleasures, for it is not what you do, it is what that does to you that truly makes life special. After travelling down a relatively straight section of the road we came to the large sweeping bend I had noticed earlier. This turned out to be even larger and longer than I had imagined from the vantage point we had paused at, now miles behind. Bedding down aerodynamically into the frame I attacked the road with the fury and might of a god, rounding the apex at an incredible speed. A speed more worthy of my little blue sports car, or a pro athlete, not a man of dubious fitness on a budget bicycle. For a brief moment, I felt truly powerful.

Further down the road I could see we were approaching a little hamlet of a handful of small cottages which lined the road side. As we came close to the first house I began to see the population of the village were stepping out of their houses. The older folk sat on their doorstep leisurely enjoying a French café in the late morning sun, as the local children grouped together with their friends playing games up and down the street. As our bikes passed the threshold of the village, I was witness to yet another reason why I am now convinced a push bike is by far the greatest method of transport on which to travel through France. With smiling faces the entire population of this tiny village clapped, cheered and waved us on through like we were celebrities. Now I understand that cycling is popular in France due in part to events such as the TDF (Tour de France) but respect for cyclists of all fitness levels seems so widespread amongst the whole population regardless of how rural or how urbanised. To be in receipt of this love and admiration first hand was an amazing experience, almost a spiritual feeling that I will treasure for the rest of my life.

The miles ticked on as the beautiful ever changing scenery passed, soon enough we were approaching our first lunch point of the French side of our journey.

Our lunch stop was to be found in another little French village only this one was remarkably different than the last; as we cycled through it was eerily quiet and seemingly empty with little to no sign that anyone was either awake or at home at all. Slowly our bikes crawled through, making as little noise as possible as if trying not to disturb the slightly unnerving stillness of the place like it was something out of the pages of a zombie apocalypse story. That was until the silence was broken forcefully by the savage and authoritative bark of a large black guard dog, woken from its slumber by the smell, sound and eventual sight of over a hundred cyclists passing by his sentry post as he lay on the ground behind a fence guarding what seemed to be a non-operational pottery or stone mason's workshop with its army of gargoyles, grotesques, and pile after pile of roofing tiles. At the request of one of our orange route markers we turned left off the main road at a near hairpin steep bend on to a road that seemed to take us in the general direction we had just come from but not for any great distance till we were instructed to turn right on to a little grass playing field that ran alongside a fenced off children's play park with a large climbing frame and a couple of swing sets. The field was littered with the cyclists from our route either laying on the grass in their individual little groups chatting while soaking up the sun or hiding in the shade of the odd tree or bush which speckled the edges of the area. Once again there was the sight of a small gazebo and support van with its now seemingly customary range of fruits, pasta dishes, chicken and finally chocolate desserts. Resting my bike on the ground by the fence I made my way straight to the food being the eating machine I am. After filling a paper plate to potentially disastrous levels of towering piles of food I stepped out from under the gazebo to the sight of cyclist resting against one of a pair of football goal posts I had previously been unaware of, which explained the function of this seemingly abandoned grass area positioned in parallel with a rubber floored children's play park. Returning to my cycling partners I made short work of consuming my plate of food and even went for a second round before refilling my water bottles and collecting a tracker bar and jelly babies to fill the pocket in the back of my jersey. A number of the groups that had been lying on the grass when we had arrived had already departed when Ajay suggested that we should not rest too long as the day was far from over and we still had many miles to cover before we reached our overnight stop. Having finished my food, I picked up my bike from the floor, stretched, and applied another dollop of tiger balm to my quads before mounting the shiny metal beast and gently guiding her back down the path to the roadside, ready to set off once more. Together the four of us rode out like a modern take on the horsemen of the apocalypse, albeit none of us actually on horseback and three of the four riding transport of the same colour, none of which could breathe fire without drinking dangerous amounts of tequila and playing with matches. The route was somewhat disorientating to begin with, first we had to turn left back on the road that had brought us to the park and cycle slightly uphill back toward the hairpin-like bend where this side of the road met the road through the village, once again disturbing the slumbering guardian of the pottery who just as before began to bark and growl, making sounds that cut through the near silence of the village like a hot knife disturbs a block of chilled butter. Pressing forward, leaving the dog and its pottery behind, we came to a sight which fitted my feeling of the place to perfection; an old and somewhat dilapidated red brick wall which in turn revealed an a wide opening about halfway along its length. As we approached the opening it was clear to see that it was in fact the badly overgrown entrance to a garage or car port which loosely speaking housed an equally dilapidated badly rusting and weed infested French automobile, all covered in moss with no sign of use or maintenance for a considerable length of time. Being the car nut I am I felt the need to slow and take in this sight, as it seemed so dug in and rooted in the living landscape of this seemingly desolate and abandoned place that it felt like some sort of shrine to social degradation, as if it was pointing to a bleak post-apocalyptic future.

As the miles cracked on the images of the sleeping village fell to the back of my mind and the scenery returned to the slightly brighter more floral lined hamlets and villages I had experienced earlier in the day. The only major difference was in the topic of conversation. Since we had arrived in France the conversation had often been defined by the environment we were cycling through at the time. At the time in question we had just spent a couple of hours cycling past some farming communities and several fields of cut crops and the sight of hay bales dotted the vista to the left and right. But as we soldiered on towards our next water stop the names of the nearby villages gave rise to lots of laughter and innuendo from all of us. Names such as Assenhim, cummenhim, and mingeoval (at least that was they sounded like!), which I have no doubt are perfectly innocent and normal when said in French, but can be given very rude if not outright offensive meanings when said in English. These crude jokes continued for many miles getting progressively more drawn out and stretched until we saw another group of cyclists from our route come out from a little French café. The sight of this reminded me of how unfit I actually was and made us realise that had we been of a higher level of fitness and physique we would have naturally carried a slightly higher cadence and therefore a slightly higher average ground covering speed. This in turn would have meant that we would have had more chance to stop and interact with some of the communities we had been cycling through, or arrive at our pre planned stops earlier. As I hope to have shown throughout this book, life often isn't about the destination, its more about the journey you take to get there. As I always tell people that I meet, it's not **what you do** it's what **it does to you** that matters.

We crossed a small bridge over a small stream and continued down a relatively long straight road. This road eventually led us to our next water stop.

As we came around a corner we saw a little wayhead, a sort of layby or at least an undefined area of dusty ground that ran along beside the road, and the now familiar sight of the other cyclists on our route all grouped together by one of the support vans which was parked in the layby. As we approached I could see that the area backed on to some sort of grassland field bordered on two sides by trees and hedgerows, and a waist height wooden fence along the side closest to us. Slowing to a scooting pace we gently passed everyone who was already standing around chatting near to the back of the van, to add our bikes to the end of the line resting against the fence in the shade of the very large old tree which was growing near to but on the other side of the fence. Feeling well practiced at the drill we signed in and began to mingle with the other cyclists. After making casual small talk for a little while I then felt an extreme and undeniable need to urinate. Realising that we were probably several miles from a public convenience I felt glad that I was both male and of a mind-set that I feel comfortable with nature and survival in the wild. Clambering quickly over the low fence I discreetly made my way over to the shadowed side of the large tree that was providing shade for our bikes. Using the tree trunk as cover to conceal my actions I wrestled with my clothing until I had successfully exposed myself and began to relieve my bladder pressure against the bark of the trunk till I found I had created an odourless translucent pool of pale yellowish liquid on the floor by the root of a quite colossal living timber. Once again I wrestled with my clothing and once appropriately covered I returned to the group.

I did this with expert timing which concealed my actions, allowing my call of nature to pass unnoticed by the majority of the group. I reassumed my previous position at the rear of the crowd, to listen to the next announcement from the support staff. As we listened we were informed that the crew up ahead had run in to difficulties with the local populous who were objecting to the placement of our route-marking orange arrows. This information was however, passed on in such an innuendo sounding way that it caused a wave of uncontrollable laughter to wash over the group. The exact words that caused this commotion were "We seem to be having trouble putting arrows up in Arras" which when pronounced in English sounded like 'her ass'. Once the giggling and shouts of "you need lubrication honey!" had died down he continued to explain that once again we were split over two hotels, an Ibis and a Mercure, with rough directions to each, and that once we had all checked in, it would be time for dinner. With the information received everyone returned to their bikes and slowly the groups started to depart. Returning to our bikes, my cycling companions and I disembarked. Down the road a little way we had begun to split into two pairs as it seemed that Ajay and I were unable to keep pace with Harshal and Abrar who had started to race each other over a series of short sprints. This gap became a problem as we came around couple of hairpin bends down a small hillside to the base of a valley. Harshal and Abrar were too far ahead for us to inform them that they had potentially taken the wrong path at a fork in the road, thanks to my eagle eye detecting that the arrow they had followed pointing up the other side of the valley was a forgery and that the real one had been partially obscured by a broken tree branch. This was proven to be fact by the support staff when I dialled the emergency contact number. The correct route was along the valley floor and ran adjacent to the side wall of a beautifully well maintained graveyard. We waited by the now uncovered arrow and spent a few moments trying unsuccessfully to phone our missing friends. Having no luck in making contact we were advised to carry on and head for our destination and hoped that we'd meet up with our missing partners somewhere along the way. Weather wise, the cycling conditions that afternoon were perfect as we cycled down the road that ran parallel with the graveyard boundary; the sun was bright but the wind cool and crisp. The tarmac was smooth and intermittently shaded from direct sunlight by an overhanging treeline of continually varied density. Further good fortune fell upon us as we reached the end of the road. The mouth of the road widened and sloped off to one side as it met a wide and seemingly major road that was, at that moment, incredibly quiet. We spotted one of the orange route marking arrows. This was situated directly opposite in the mouth of another road which was the mirror image of where we had emerged from and so instructed us to carefully time a dash straight across the road and travel down the mirror image. Before we had even made it all the way across, I noticed in the corner of my eye the sight of Harshal and Abrar pedalling their way down the main road towards us; as we had converged by the orange arrow we scooted to a stop some 150 yards clear of the junction to take a moment's rest so that we could hear all about how Harshal and Abrar had not noticed that they had gone wide of the mark till they almost ended up on a duel carriageway, and then how they had found their way back to us by more luck than judgement as they had not been able to fully retrace all of their steps.

Once the four of us were again underway cycling together it was not long till we hit the edge of suburbia and the outskirts the town of Arras, which ended the trail of orange arrows as we had been informed. Unfortunately thanks to the events that had unfolded since gaining such information none of us could remember clearly how we were supposed to traverse the town, all that I could recall was that the train station was an important waypoint; the problem was finding it as we had emerged out on to at complex but small and very busy roundabout with a petrol station opposite and a corner shop and café off to our right. Having only limited French between us, we couldn't find any signage we could understand and nothing seemed to mention 'la gare'. Parking our bikes carefully against a wall Harshal and I stood guard as Ajay and Abrar disappeared into the shop to ask for directions from a local resident. While they were inside Harshal and I watched the traffic, as we did so we also watched two more cyclists from our route navigate their way through the traffic and disappear in the direction of the centre of the town. Emerging from the shop doorway Abrar and Ajay quickly informed us that thanks to a bit of a language barrier they were not much wiser than before entering the shop, however upon hearing correlation between what Harshal and I had witnessed and that which Abrar and Ajay had been told we decided that we had a rough direction in which to initially travel and that as long as we took it slowly and steadily we should be able to 'fly blind' as the saying goes. Although it's not a method of travel I would normally recommend this haphazard hit and hope approach to route planning actually worked in our favour; turning off of a main street we dismounted and pushed our bikes down an alleyway which ran alongside of a beautiful big building of very grand architecture in a gothic and monastic style. At the end of the alley we walked back out of the shadows in to the light of large open rectangular town square bordered on three sides with vibrant semi open-fronted cafes and restaurants and the occasional gift shop, selling all the items the uneducated of the British populous wrongly stereotype French culture to revolve around. For example, black brie and blue and white horizontal striped shirts. The fourth and closest side of this beautiful paved community space was completely taken up by the impressive vista of the cathedral-like building we had just walked out from beside. Walking along one side of the rectangle towards the opposite end, Harshal and I noted a sign hanging from the side of a building; the building was on a corner of the square and the sign was hanging two of three storeys up in the air down an alleyway which sort of mirrored the one we had entered from. This sign was for the Ibis hotel where Harshal and I were due to be spending the night. It was at this point that the four of us agreed we would be best off to split back in to two twos as it was pointless Harshal and I continuing to find our way to the Mercure via the train station only to then go back and forth between the Ibis and the Mercure, first to drop our stuff off and check in and then for dinner when we were already there, so could get settled in and make our way over for dinner with everyone else later. Walking into the hotel reception, pushing our bikes along beside us, we were greeted by a member of the hotel staff who was sitting behind the small and quite cramped looking reception desk, and a member of our support staff, who jumped up from his chair by the elevator and congratulated us on completing the day's cycle, informing us that our luggage had already been checked in to our room, waiting for us. He gestured around the corner and explained that our bikes would be spending their evening outside in the restful little courtyard garden in the centre of the hotel. As we pushed our bikes through the breakfast room toward the garden doors we were greeted by a couple of the other cyclists from our group who had arrived at the evening's destination in such good time that they had time to sit in the breakfast room a while and enjoy a couple of French patisseries and a coffee. Jumping from their seats to kindly greet us they were keen to enquire about how the journey had been today as my bike and its rather extensive list of tyre inner tube replacements had for all the wrong reasons made me quite the celebrity amongst the group. I reassured them that I was fine and that despite the technical difficulties the bike and I were in good spirits and were happy to soldier on toward Paris the following day. Walking out in to the courtyard garden I spotted a gap by some steps, I chained our bikes to a wall-mounted hand rail and propped them up against the wall, before we ventured upstairs to our room, as we had only an hour and twenty minutes before we had to leave for dinner at the other hotel.

After the perfectly comfortable but simple level of refinement of our previous night's accommodation, the Ibis was a small but expected let down being that it is known to be the more budget brand. Our standard twin room was tiny to the extreme with barely three inches of room in between our single beds, and only about six inches between the beds and the wall either side with very faded peach and green woodchip wallpaper. After deciding who was to take which bed we placed our phones on charge, our wallets on the virtually non-existent bedside tables and laid back on our beds to watch a couple of minutes of some international news program on the television screwed to the wall in between the two chests of drawers at the foot of the beds. Once we had topped up our knowledge on a couple of world events we decided who was going to be allowed to use the tiny shower room first as we needed to get ready for dinner. Harshal used the shower before me which gave me time to pick my phone up and use the hotel's Wi-Fi connection to send Rosie and my family a couple of messages informing them of the day's events and that I had safely arrived at our second night stop. Once we were both showered and suitably dressed for dinner Harshal and I made our way downstairs to meet with our peers and the staff who were to lead us on a couple of minute walk over to the Mercure to join the other half of the cyclists and enjoy our first proper French meal together. leaving the Ibis through the main entrance but this time baring left to walk behind the adjacent shops, we walked in to a small courtyard which seemed quite a shocking sight as it looked more like it belonged in the east end of London, not a French market town in the middle of northern France. It was decorated like a scene from EastEnders, with a couple of benches, British lettering style road signs, an old fashioned red phone box, and even a Royal Mail post box. It was such a bizarre little place to find such a setting, unfortunately I did not have time to find my smart phone to take a picture as we were unsure as to how long the walk to the other hotel would take, in reality I could have stopped and taken a few snaps but

I wasn't to know this at the time. Arriving a few minutes earlier than expected we were required to spend a couple of minutes standing out on the pavement in front of the hotel before venturing inside. During this time there was lots of small talk about whether or not we should be collecting souvenirs from each of our stops or saving our spending money for our day in Paris at the conclusion of the event. Everyone had a different opinion and it was a good light hearted discussion about everyone's thoughts; one gentleman explained that the only items he would not be able to return home without were a couple of French brie for his daughters. With this the time quickly passed and we were taken inside to meet the others, some of whom had been propping up the bar so to speak as they were only required to take an elevator up to their rooms if they felt that the day was complete after dinner. Walking in to the dining room, we saw several large round tables each one capable of sitting approximately sixteen people. With no set seating plan we were left to mingle and sit where we felt comfortable. I prefer to sit against a wall rather than have my back facing the centre of the room and so as the tables began to fill I took a seat at one adjacent to the side wall of the rectangular room. My cycling friends took the seats to my right leaving the rest of the circle to my left to slowly be filled by the other cyclists, most of whom seemed to be traveling in either pairs or threesomes. Once we were all seated waitresses and waiters came around and took drink orders. Our dinner that evening consisted of a vegetable soup starter, followed by a grilled chicken breast with steamed veg including broccoli and carrots, with potatoes a creamy onion sauce and French bread. This was followed by a small fruity pastry dessert. All of which tasted very pleasant but the portion sizes left me feeling somewhat still hungry by the end of the meal. There was a short presentation by the support staff to explain roughly how far we had come since leaving London and the type of altitudes we had climbed to in order to mount the hills we had cycled over the last couple of days. They also explained that in the following morning those of us staying over at the Ibis would be convoyed over to the Mercure so that we could all depart together from the car park at the rear of the hotel, and finally that rest of the evening was ours if we wished to take a small walk around the centre of Arras before turning in for the evening. As we departed the dining room I was informed that I was not the only one who felt that dinner, albeit lovely, was not quite fully filling, leading to Harshal, Abrar, Ajay and myself agreeing that the four of us would take a gentle walk with the intention of finding somewhere that looked nice to have some more food. Leaving their hotel and walking back in the direction of ours we quickly found ourselves back in the square where we split up earlier. Walking out of the square via the corner closest to our hotel we came across some roadworks which partially blocked both the road and the pavement. Crossing the road to avoid the maintenance work we came across a man who looked to be a tramp, sitting in an old badly maintained brown overcoat, on the middle of a wide but short set of stone steps leading to a row of shops with what looked to be either hotel rooms or apartments above. As we passed he overheard our chatter about food. Pointing over his shoulder he gestured in the direction of the far end of the rank of shops and proclaimed that we would find the greatest American style burger joint in the town up there. Talking amongst ourselves we decided that we would wander up the way and take a look even though we would have preferred to find somewhere with a more healthy sounding menu. As it was, upon our arrival at the end of the row we found the place had shut for the night a few moments earlier. Taking that as some sort of good omen we turned around and walked back towards the steps before walking further on past the road works. We came across an Indian restaurant but decided to continue to search for somewhere different as two of my cycling friends were of Indian descent and the third was of Pakistani heritage. Soon enough we came across a small restaurant which turned out to be a French run Italian. The place looked popular, comfortable, clean and tidy, and I guess a sort of passionate little family run enterprise. The place reminded me of Settantanove in Ilfracombe High Street, the local pizzeria I regularly took Rosie to. Stepping inside, the four of us were shown to a table near to a little ornate arch which split the room into two halves. At the back of the restaurant there was a short bar in front of a little recess in the back wall which housed a collection of wine and spirit bottles arranged over a couple of shelves. Either side of the bar there was a door. One side was for the kitchen, and the other side for the toilet. The staff seemed to consist of a young girl of mid to late teenage years, and an attractive woman who I guess would have been in her mid-thirties. They were busy, efficiently waiting on the tables, and it did not take long before it was our turn to give our drinks order. We had chosen to have soft drinks and a jug of water on the table as none of our four wanted to develop a hangover as we knew we had another long day in the saddle starting the following morning, which would have been an unsurmountable challenge with a pounding headache and a churning stomach. Moments later our waitress returned with our drinks and enquired as to our food order. From our brief inspection of the menu we were fully prepared for her enquiry as we had chosen to share a couple of pizzas with some garlic bread. It was not long before our food arrived and we began to tuck in to what were two very tasty crispy based pizzas and the bread. As the conversation about the day's events, sights and sounds flowed between us, so did the humorous fact that from a third person perspective we were like the beginning of a bad joke, which would start along lines of: two Indians, a Pakistani and an Englishman attempted to cycle to Paris…

At the end of our meal we each pulled out our wallets with which to pay the bill and started counting out money. In turn, we each passed a small handful of bank notes to Abrar who had been the one doing the ordering and so was also the person who had asked for the bill. Once the bill was paid we swiftly left but not before I had chance to exercise a little demon of mine for turning paper napkins in to paper roses which in the past I have either given to a beautiful lady right there and then, or during times of my life when I have a significant other who could not be present at the moment in question, taken said flower home to her as a romantic gesture. Some guys bring their loved ones bunches of cut flowers, I make them one. Leaving the restaurant we walked back the way we came. This time when we got to the big main square I stopped and quickly remembered to pull out my smartphone to get a couple of pictures of the beautiful architecture to help explain the beauty of the architecture I had experienced. As it was getting really late and we were pleasantly stuffed we decided once again to split in to our two twos and head for our respective hotels. In hindsight, I regrettably have to admit that I forgot to suggest we go in search of the little courtyard that had perplexed me with its seemingly English furniture. It wasn't long before Harshal and I crashed in through the door of our hotel room and collapsed on our beds. After a few minutes laying there we each in turn found the energy to get back up and use the bathroom to prepare for bed properly. As I got into bed and settled down for the night I plugged my phone charger in, briefly took a look through my photos and lastly began to think once again of my love and how I missed her being laid next to me snoring away; it was always a race between us as to who could fall asleep first as the other would have to put up with horrendous noisy snoring for potentially hours to come, and so I resolved my feelings to send Rosie a text message just to say simply 'I love you, good night.'

Chapter Twenty
Day Three: Arras to Compiègne

Awaking in the morning light I felt suitably refreshed enough to take on the day's ride, this was the last of the full day rides and was the shortest of the three, weighing in at approximately eighty miles. Sitting upright in our beds Harshal and I agreed that as budget as the room's décor and furniture were, we had been able to sleep to an arguably satisfactory standard. The lack of additional comfort also made for easy rising from our beds once we had discussed the order of who would get to use the bathroom first and what time we were both to be ready by to go downstairs for breakfast. Steadily we took turns to clean our teeth, shower and in my case comb my hair and beard, a time constraint that Harshal did not have to deal with, being a man whom it was clear regularly attacked, or paid someone else to attack the top and bottom of his skull with a razor, albeit very gently and with what must be pin point, or should I say knife edge precision and accuracy. With all things hair related dealt with and while Harshal was using the bathroom I proceeded to once again liberally smoothen the inside of my legs with chamois butter and apply tiger balm to my calf muscles, taking great care to not to cross contaminate or mix up the two products knowing all too well the hours of pain and burning sensation that can be caused by red tiger balm coming in contact with the more private areas of the male anatomy. Once fully lubricated I began to dress, first in a pair of my padded cycling shorts, with a quick squirt of deodorant under the arm pits and down the front of my shorts, then I turned my attention to the top half of my body swiftly pulling on one of my retina scorching bright neon yellow tops. Once we were both fully clean, dressed and prepped for the day ahead we took a couple of moments to each check our packing and inspect the room for any stray items of our luggage. Satisfied that all we were leaving behind was dead skin cells, fallen hair and bacteria we folded our bed sheets in to neat pile ready for collection by housekeeping and left our room carrying our baggage downstairs to the breakfast room, to use the term lightly. As we entered the room at one end and could see it was arranged as a number of long tables stretching across the centre of the room placed side by side down the length of the room towards the glass wall view of the courtyard garden. On the near side wall of the rectangular space were a couple of small tables intended for individual couples or lone travellers. On the other side of the room, running along the length of the opposite side wall, was large and substantially supported shelf which housed tray after tray of breakfast items in a continental style; jugs of orange, apple, and grapefruit juice. Kettles sat in front of small baskets of assorted teabags, regularly replaced pots of fresh coffee, Fruit, cereals, and French patisseries. It was a large but simple spread of all the items one associates with breakfast when staying in a French hotel or guest house. Nothing particularly flashy or impressive, just all the basic elements done to a satisfactory standard. Following Harshal I collected one of the small plastic trays and a plate from their respective stacks at the end of the shelf and worked my way along, collecting a small glass of fruit juice followed by some toast, a croissant and finally an English breakfast tea; I am a proud Englishman after all and not much of a coffee drinker. Feeling like that was enough for my first trip we sat down and tucked in to round one. Sitting down I noticed two things, the first being that the plastic chairs were similar to the ones you would find in the classrooms of most English secondary schools, fine for short periods of sitting but not all that comfortable, feeling slightly on the flimsy side, but nonetheless constructed well enough to support the weight of most adult men when used in the proper manner. The other draw of my attention was that for the second morning we had purely by chance timed our breakfast in sync with that of the muscular tattooed Kiwi fella on our route. Conversation about the previous day's cycling and our thoughts and feelings about that day's oncoming challenges reverberated round the room between everyone's mouthfuls of breakfast. It wasn't long till I was required by my gut to rise from my seat and circle the room for a second tray of food, this time sampling the second option of juice and taking a small glass of milk due to my need for only one cup of tea to awaken my senses on a morning. This was shortly followed by a final third tray before I felt that I had reached the crossroads of either being not full but discreetly fed, or looking like a glutton going for a fourth tray, therefore rude and unpatriotic to my country of origin and upbringing. With our breakfast completed, a few at a time we took it in turns to walk out to the courtyard garden and collect our bikes. As I knelt down to unchain my bike I heard the sound of someone wrestling with a bike behind me. Returning to my feet and turning to face the commotion I was met by the sight of the Kiwi fella lifting his bike clear from being trapped behind another that was sandwiched between it and the wall. Placing the bike on the ground in front of him and letting the saddle lean against his thigh he cursed under his breath, and with a sort of morbid humour in his voice he addressed his bike. "Right you little bitch, are you going to be nice or are you going to try and kill me again today?" Realising that given our proximity there was a high probability that I would have overheard him, he explained how he had quite spectacularly come flying off or been injured while using the bike. Upon closer inspection I became quickly aware of the perilous and exhausting reality he was enduring. Compared to mine, His bike was somewhat more expensively constructed in terms of materials used to form the frame and wheels, but was from a mechanical or engineering view point a much simpler design. My bike, as I have explained previously, was an old fashioned but effective Shimano index system of seven on the rear and two in front giving me effectively fourteen gears to choose from when finding the correct gear for the road conditions and my fitness. On the other hand his bike was a single fixed gear arrangement. Having no derailleur this produced multiple problems for him. The first being that no matter how steep or conversely how flat the road conditions he was limited to only having the one gear to use for all situations. When out on my bike if I decide not to pedal due to feeling exhausted or traveling downhill, I can stop pedalling, the gears disengage and the rear wheel can continue to turn freely. On his, the drive could not be disengaged meaning the pedals have to turn with the rear wheel no matter what. Furthermore if he was to take his foot off, the pedal would continue to rotate potentially causing it to make contact with and rip painfully in to his calf muscle. To stop this from happening no matter how tired and exhausted the rides made him feel he had to keep his legs in motion and keep pedalling. Reassuring him that if the roles were reversed he would have heard me saying something similar we laughed and wheeled our bikes inside to collect our baggage. Handing our keys back and officially checking out of our rooms, we made our way outside to the front of our hotel where we grouped ready to walk our bikes over to the other hotel to meet with the other cyclists and head off on the third day of our adventure. Getting to the Mercure, we were instructed to wheel our bikes around the side of the building and meet with the other half of the group in the large public car park to the rear of the hotel; as we did so one of the support team was a little worried about my rear tyre looking a little flat and so once signed in he took me to one side and checked my tyre pressure, this turn out to read 99psi when the tyre recommended 100psi so it was decided that I was fine to ride the first section of the day and that he would check it again at the water stop, even if I had not noticed any change. With the mechanical check out of the way I set off, now cycling a fair few minutes behind Abrar and Ajay, with basically no hope of catching up before the morning stop. I was however mere seconds behind Harshal, and so pushing on hard I was able to catch up with my roommate by the time we reached the outskirts of the town, where the flat ground began to snake up a beautiful tree-lined hill climb which seemed to be never ending, just getting steeper and steeper after every turn of a corner only to momentarily flatten out slightly between them. Feeling out of breath and struggling to keep up the pace we had previously cycled at, Harshal and I could afford little in the way of conversation as we climbed, in turn muttering just one short sentence every few hundred yards; "at least it's nice scenery" or "yeah, my Mazda would love it here" are good examples of our laboured communications. Reaching the summit of the climb we refrained for a moment, looking over our shoulders at the town we had spent the night in. Once again focusing on the journey ahead we noticed that the terrain had almost completely flattened out for the next stretch and off in the middle distance had started to even fall away, signalling a downwards slope for us to gather some speed during the descent. A little way further down the road, and fortunately at a point where we had settled down in to our saddles and were cruising along at a comfortably quick pace, we came across the official photographer who was again taking action shots as people rode past him. Harshal and I, both wanting to look our best, took up determined forceful poses and facial expressions, eyebrows low, little wry smiles, chests pushed out, leaning forward on the bikes. We kept these poses till we felt safe in the idea that we were no longer in sight of the photographer and his lens. Shortly, we came to a descending slope of the earlier horizon. The descent was short and uneventful. Soon we were cycling quickly through wide open farmland and once again I was reminded of my local cycle routes I had used to make up the majority of my training. It can be said the climate and landscape of northern France is very similar to that of the counties of Devon and Somerset. To begin with the sky was overcast with clouds but generally bright, but as we cycled the clouds got progressively more dense and the wind changed from a gentle air of mild cooling still, into the occasional alarming stab of cold chilling gust. This short and subtle trend toward heavier weather soon broke in to a thankfully brief downpour of cold rain, from which I had little protection wearing only a thin layer of breathable Lycra. Within seconds the only part of my body that wasn't soaking wet was, to my shock, my feet. It transpired that my cheap and unstylish trainers were in fact fairly water resistant. However this was only briefly an advantage as water began to trickle down the skin of my leg and reach my sock which acted like a sponge, meaning that soon my strangely waterproof footwear was filling with water from the inside, which in turn had no means of escape. Steadily I squelched on through the rain, determined to not let it dampen my mood as well as my body, until the clouds broke and the morning sun came blazing through. Within moments of being back in the direct sunlight my Lycra clothing was steaming as it quickly lost all the excess moisture and dried out. Unfortunately my shoes were much slower at this but given time even they returned to their previous condition. Happily we cycled on but I found myself watchfully monitoring the sky up ahead, wanting to be pre-warned of another shower as far in advance as possible. At times we cycled through damp areas of ground that had not long before seen heavy rainfall but none fell upon my head. Shortly later we rounded a corner by a large tree and found that we had gained on and caught up with Abrar and Ajay who had stopped briefly a couple of times that morning to sequentially unpack and then repack their wet weather gear in answer to the changing climate. The awesome foursome had regrouped and it wasn't long till the route markers took us off of the main road up a shallow curving hillside in the direction of a long line of tall trees a way off in the middle distance. The tree line was a good couple of miles away but felt like it was at the correct distance to herald the coming of our water stop for the morning. Cycling on, we soon were within fifty metres of the tree line; again the route marking arrows told us to turn off the road, this time down a short but wildly snaking sort of driveway which ended up in a wide, concreted car park. On one side this was bordered neatly with high rising kerbstones leading on one edge to a grass covered picnic area. Running along the other side of the car park, dug into the ground in front of the tree line was a low slung and wide single storey building constructed of concrete at one end and mainly glass at the other. At the bottom of the car park we could see all our other cycling peers who as usual were either milling around by the support vehicles or lying on the grass having a piece of fruit and a well-earned rest for a few minutes. Once the four of us had signed in and refuelled on fruit and water we were informed of our location and offered time to take a look around and inspect the immediate area as the low slung building was the visitors' centre at the entrance to Thiepval, the memorial to the soldiers who gave their lives during the battle for the Somme valley during the Great War of 1914-1918. Upon receiving this information I quickly chained my bike to a nearby sign and headed in to the building with a very heavy sombre feeling washing over me. The inside of the building was light and airy due to large walls of glass and partially glazed roof. It had a tranquil atmosphere similar to that of a library. Posters and photos lined the walls showing images of the war and the destruction it caused, both in loss of lives and physical scarring of the landscape. In display cabinets were old weapons and mortar shells or models of the cannons themselves. There was a small glass door on the back wall that led out to a small winding garden path which headed through the trees and met a large gravel driveway that intersected with the treeline a little way to the left of the building, or ran along the tree line in the other direction with its terminal point obscured from view by the trees and the rest of the building. Approaching the door I noticed a number of multi lingual signs which seem to say 'this way to the memorial' in many of the widely used world languages. Heading out through the door and passing amongst the trees I found myself on the gravel driveway. Looking to my left all I saw was the end of the gravel where it met the car park at the side of the building. Turning to my right however I was met by the irreverent and majestic sight of the memorial itself. There it stood tall against the blue sky of a French midsummer's day. Mounted on of a platform constructed of both red brick and large sections of white smooth faced stonework stood sixteen tall flat faced rectangular pillars of the same white stonework. These were arranged as four sets of fours in a square made of other smaller squares. These were in turn capped at the top with more brickwork and stonework to make two archways, one which faced north to south and one east to west but they were all connected at the central point of the monument. Crowning the roof of the monument were two short flagpoles from which flew, on the left hand side, the Union Jack of the United Kingdom of Great Britain, and by its side on the right hand flagpole, the Tricolour of France. As we approached the monument I could feel a great turbulence of mixed emotions. The size and subtle elegant splendour of the architecture gave a feeling of importance, which although mixed with the quite irreverent, still produced an image that would have been fitting of an ancient religious site. Once standing amongst the pillars at the centre of the monument it was easy to make out the thousands of names carefully carved into each and every face of the pillars. These names were those of the men who had not returned from or had lost their lives during the battle for the Somme and the other trench warfare campaigns of the time. This was one of the most drawn out and destructive conflicts of the Great War. Reading some of the names from the closest pillar I began to feel a sympathetic sadness for the families of the names I had seen as they would have gone through a terrible pain, losing a brother, a father, or a son, possibly in the prime of life. This was a feeling that I found difficult to truly comprehend in its entirety. At the time my father was still alive and for the most part well, and my experience with death within the family was limited to the passing of my grandparents, the loss of which had been hard to deal with but not as hard as the pain I felt at my father's passing on a couple of years later. At the time, as I was standing in the monument I did however feel lucky on two counts, the first being that I had not lost a member of my immediate family, and the second being thankful for the knowledge that my ancestors, who had seen military duty during the Great War, had returned home, and so would not be found carved into the pillars of the memorial's stone records. One such ancestor on my mother's side of my family tree had indeed been part of the battle for the Somme but, due to his beliefs and opinions, had not been there in a combat role. Instead he was sent out on to the battlefield after the day's fighting to collect the dead and wounded in a sort of humanitarian capacity. In my mind, this was noble undertaking, and I had lot of pride in the image of a man with enough inner steel and a strong enough sense of moral code that he refused to take the life of another man simply because he was told to, and instead was present simply to support and care for his fellow man during their time of need. Equally a counterpart on my father's side of the family tree was, during that time, part of the coastguard and so was stationed as part of a three man team at the lookout on Morte Point, near the tiny north Devon coastal village of Mortehoe and the beautiful beach resort that is the village of Woolacombe. As I looked around the monument I also surveyed the rows of tiny white crosses like anonymous unmarked gravestones stretching out in all directions around the monument. Soon I realised that I had spent quite a long time lost in the enchantment of the place and that it was time to return to my bike, not wishing to lag behind or give myself an even larger task of keeping pace during the next segment of the day. This turned out to be like some sort of strange premonition as a few miles down the road my rear tyre blew out for the third or possibly fourth time; it had happened so many times I was beginning to lose track of how many inner tubes I had actually gone through. Feeling like a bit of burden on my cycling partners, and sounding sort of like an American soldier in a Vietnam War film I instructed Harshal and the others to go on without me, 'I'll meet you at the lunch stop when I can!' This actually turned in to quite a serendipitous occurrence as once my bike and I were mobile again I had no chance of properly catching up to my friends before the stop for lunch. I was forced to use my powers of extreme social openness to introduce myself to and start a conversation with a different couple of cyclists from our route. The couple I ended up cycling with during that section of the day were an older married couple nearing retirement who had decided that they wanted to do something different with their allotted time and budget they had set aside for a foreign holiday. So instead of the normal practices of their peers such as flying to Rome or Paris for a long weekend and then flying home, or alternatively taking short cruise from Southampton or Norfolk over to the Nordic fjords or the Med, they had wanted a more exciting adventurous holiday and also an opportunity to raise money for a good charitable cause. Through a few days of internet research they had discovered the London to Paris cycling challenge. They had then decided that it was the perfect answer to the question of what to do with their holidays that year, as it combined their first two constraints with a test of fitness and physical conditioning. With the decision made they had signed up and paid their entrance fees, with the exception of a little retained for souvenir shopping and enjoying the day in Paris at the end of the ride. They had donated all the money they would have spent booking an average cruise ship holiday to Action Medical Research, and began to train for the event. Cycling with them was a slightly slower and therefore far less physically demanding pace than I had been used to during the previous couple of days. This was due in part to their bikes, these were expensive hybrid bikes that mixed a road bike frame and tyre and gear change system with a cushioned comfortable saddle and suspension set up you would find on a good mountain bike. The concept behind the production of these bikes was to create a vehicle that was comfortable being used in both branches of cycling. This however had turned out to be an object that fell between two stools, being OK but not great at either. The engineers and designers had overcome the problem I had experienced using a mountain bike on the road by building a lock out function to the suspension to stop it from sapping the pedal power while hill climbing on solid surfaces. Unfortunately for the gentleman I was cycling with the lock out function of his bike had failed and so he was back to the draining task fighting against the suspension at every hill climb. This slow but steady pace gave us lots of time to discuss a great list of different topics such as cycling training and preparation for the journey; it was soon clear that once again I had undertaken far less than this near retirement couple had. To my credit however it was clear in this case that I had the exuberance of youth on my side as although they were in very good health and impressive physical condition when compared to other people of their age, physical performance wise they were no challenge for a man of my age. Feeling like our progress was little too slow I began to thinking about how far it was till the lunch stop and my opportunity to continue on with Harshal and the guys as I had previously become accustomed. Snapping back to reality I felt the bike slip underneath me slightly as the ground changed to a slightly smoother surface like polished concrete. Looking around me it seemed as though the road actually cut through a large well-maintained but somewhat quiet and restful farmyard with long stone walled agricultural looking buildings immediately either side of the road set in well-tended grass fields, with massive muddy tyre tracks which crisscrossed the path between them. At this point in our ride together my current cycling partners started taking an interest in my life and asked me questions about my personal triumphs to date, such as my degree, as well as enquiring about my life goals and dreams for the future and so I spent a mile or two talking about my most expert subject, myself. Soon the landscape changed once again, becoming a large, relatively flat open plain scarred with the occasional crater of seemingly massive sections of ground torn up. The sky directly above was a pale grey but up ahead on the horizon dark clouds amassed and the air felt razor sharp and seemed to tingle with an electrical charge as if the flash of lightening and the roll of thunder were an ever present threat. Glancing over my shoulder I realised the sky back the way we had just come from was turning equally dark and thunderous, as if we were actually present in the calm at the eye of a great storm. As we cycled on, the ground in front became increasingly damper as if it had not long seen rainfall but still my head remained dry. Another couple of miles down the path we came in sight of the lunch stop. As we approached we could make out the support van parked underneath a couple of large trees by a T junction where the road we were currently on met another and ended. The closer we came the more drowned our fellow cyclists looked. Pulling up underneath the trees we were greeted by everyone who was happy to see us and glad to see that my bike was still soldiering on in spite of the recurring issues it suffered from. After signing in I was reunited with Harshal, Ajay, and Abrar who informed me that the conditions they had cycled through were, as I suspected, torrential rain and winds more fitting to a tropical storm. Once I had refuelled my water bottles, my belly and relieved my bladder behind a bulbous bush-like plant nearby, I was ready and joining Abrar, Harshal, and Ajay in saying farewell to the lunch stop, the awesome foursome joined the next little wave of cyclists to depart heading off on the next leg of the day's journey. Up ahead I could see the road began to descend down a hillside away from the plain, and before we were lost from view I turned back to wave at the cyclists still at the lunch stop. As I did so the clouds immediately above surrounding the trees they were all standing under opened up and released a downpour of rain water that pounded the ground so hard it looked like it recoiled back up in to the air by a metre or two. Harshal looked over at me and said "We had better keep moving, I don't want that to catch up with us." This refocused me on the road ahead and how it was beginning to have intermittent shelter provided by patches of dense tree cover to the right of the road in a similar manner to the graveyard we had passed the previous afternoon. The big difference was that in this instance the road was running down the side of a huge battle scarred valley, not a quite well-tended cemetery. As we cycled along, the four of us sequentially merged with and then split from a couple of other groups who had departed at the same time. This was governed by the natural cycling speed adopted by the individual groups and the length of time they spent stopped at one of the designated viewing points to get photos of the valley floor far below us. At each of these points the hedge had been cut back to reveal a wall which for the most part it obscured; the wall I guessed acted like a safety barrier stopping a reckless individual from careering off the road and falling at their peril down the steep sides of the valley. Taking the place of the hedge at these points there were slightly raised concrete platforms from which it was safe to peek over the wall without feeling like you were standing on the edge of a public road. We cycled on for miles until the valley was just a distant memory and we had ended up once again on a wide open grassland area. As we cycled we passed what seemed like some sort of military installation or maybe something to do with global positioning systems and satellite communication, judging by the large antennae and dish receptors located on the roof of a nearby small concrete building surrounded by a tall wire mesh fence. Just past this point we found a couple of other cyclists who had left the lunch stop well before we had; they were standing by the road side changing an inner tube as one of them had blown a tyre when he had failed to catch sight of some broken glass that littered the road surface like a minefield. Thankfully due to their presence by the side of the road I was alerted well in advance of the obstacle. While stopping to find out if they required assistance I scuffed my shoes across the road surface, gently kicking some of the glass on to the dusty patch of dry ground by the roadside. In doing this, I had yet again become separated from Harshal, Ajay and Abrar and found myself in the company of a cyclist of approximately the same age as me, who went by the name of Richard Hyde, who had also come adrift from his cycling companions and so had decided that I would be good to cycle with for a short while. Richard was a very keen amateur or, a closer description would be a semi pro road cyclist, who had suffered a major accident a year or two previous and was in the process of regaining his cycling performance, undertaking events such as this three and a half day jaunt to the French capital. Being that this was the shortest of the full cycling days there was another short water stop before our hotels and this was coming up soon. Unfortunately for me, my rear tyre yet again blew out even sooner, causing Richard and I to have to duck into a bus shelter to avoid another sudden downpour. While we stood there he kindly retrieved a spare inner tube from his tool kit and helped me fit it. Within seconds of inflation my front tyre decided to join in and blew its inner tube, leaving me with no option other than to call the support crew once again. I apologised to Richard who said he was happy to wait with me as he understood the frustration I was feeling from constantly changing inner tubes yet never finding anything penetrating the tyre wall to actually cause a puncture. The arrival of the support van was swift but initially brought bad news as they had fixed a large number of blow-outs that day and had already emptied their inner tube supplies till the morning. This, however, was counterbalanced by an idea one of the mechanics had upon inspecting the wheel assembly of my bike. Its type vaguely matched that of a spare bike they were carrying, as the rider who was going to be using it had been too ill and had dropped out of the event. This meant that they could be directly exchanged temporarily to allow me to continue, and so I was soon back on the road and capable of even faster flat land speed due to a combination of factors brought about by the wheel change; the tyres were of higher quality and so gripped better, allowing me to transfer more power to the road surface, and the wheel construction itself was different, meaning it was lighter. Soon we arrived at the water stop. After quickly signing in and refilling my water bottles I introduced Richard formally to Abrar, Harshal and Ajay and soon we departed as a group. It was quite clear that even with the new found speed of my temporary upgrade I had no chance of keeping up with Richard over any great distance, and so he rode off in front with the hope of meeting up with his original cycling party. The terrain had been flat for miles when we came across a sign that seemed to indicate that we were approaching a steep decline down to the town, which was our next overnight stop. As we descended through a couple of streets of houses we came to a fork in the road where we had been instructed to split back into our two pairs as once again the hotel Abrar and Ajay would be staying in was on side of the town and the hotel Harshal and I would be going to was basically on the edge of a business and retail park on the near side of town, next to major highway. As we cycled across the car park in the centre of the retail park we saw the large grey building that was to be our hotel. From the outside it looked very run of the mill and standard in an unexciting fashion, in the same way that British motorway service stations and their associated budget hotels look. The main entrance seemed to be glass double doors on the corner of the building and this was the direction which we cycled in. The hotel was one of a chain called All Seasons.

When we got to the hotel entrance we were met by the ride support staff, who took our bikes for over-night storage and then took us in through the doors to the reception of the hotel. Walking in, the hotel lobby was very modern and minimalist with one wall being glass panels; the whole area was bright to the point of having a very Spartan, almost clinical atmosphere of white walls and tiled floors with hard plastic stools and tables. The furniture was a random assortment of near translucent neon colours. The lack of soft furnishings accented by the occasional piece of wild vivid modern art all added up to give a clean but somewhat cold environment which felt almost sterile in nature. In the corner adjacent to the main doors was a small alcove with a couple of shelves and a couple of fridges behind a short length of counter top which made up the bar; a few feet further along the side wall of the space, and protruding further in to the middle of the room, was another counter top, this time concealing a desk behind it. This was the reception desk. Past the reception was a short corridor where we found elevators which took us to the bedrooms on the upper floors. Once the lift arrived on the first floor, the doors swung open to reveal another short corridor which opened out on to a narrow glass fronted balcony walkway, which looked down on the reception and seating area below. As we walked out and looked down at the reception I noticed a previously unseen notice board explaining that we needed to reassemble in the lobby at approximately half past six for the dinner arrangements for that evening. Arriving at our room we first had difficulty getting our key cards to register and open the door. Once the door was open we entered our room, marking the beginning of what would turn into a very strange experience that I had never expected. Initially walking in through the door our room had a sort of short internal corridor of pale grey walls, maybe six feet long, with a full room height vertical mirror about a foot wide at the far end, just before the room opened out in the main body of the space, where we could see a large flat panel television hanging on the wall at the foot end of the beds. Between the mirror and a clothes rail on the far wall, sitting against the wall below the television, was a narrow desk with the complimentary hot drinks tray. Stepping forth as far as the end of the corridor we found two comfortable, stylishly made, well sized, and nicely spaced beds, each with its own glass and chrome bedside shelf unit lamp and power point. Running the length of the wall above the head boards of the beds was more of the same modern art as downstairs, only this time, tonally matching the colour scheme of the soft furnishings of the room. In the middle of the far wall next to the clothes rail was a large window with lightweight curtains which gently defused the early evening sunlight in to the room. Generally feeling positive about out stylish accommodation Harshal and I quickly got to work on deciding which one of us had which bed and began to lay out our things. Turning the television on and lying back on his bed, Harshal offered for me to use the bathroom first to get ready for the evening and this is where the strangeness truly began. Being that I had the first bed as you entered the room, with Harshal having the bed closest the window, I turned 180 degrees away from him expecting to find a door into our en suite bathroom. What I was met with however was a complete transparent sliding glass door which led to an extremely brightly lit white and green tiled space, which in theory consumed about twenty-five percent of the original floor space of the room, and which housed a toilet in the centre, a shower head hanging from the wall to the right of the toilet, and a sink with a small counter top and towel rail to the left of the toilet. The sink had a small round mirror on a wall-mounted swinging arm above it. Sliding the glass door across I stepped into the space and looked around, only to realise that right where you were intended to stand while showering, the side wall of the tiled space was a solid piece of transparent glass that was directly opposite the full height mirror next to the television. I expected these glass panels to be made of that electro opaque glass that changes from completely transparent to a densely frosted effect at the flick of a switch. Unfortunately no such switch could be found anywhere inside or outside of the tiled room. These factors added together to create a situation where if you were sitting on the toilet or taking a shower, your roommate could no longer watch the television or in fact do anything other than stare out of the window if you both wanted to keep your dignity and avoid an awkward moment. Walking back out into the main room and talking this over with Harshal, we agreed that no matter how close we had become over the last three days we were two heterosexual Brits who both had stunningly beautiful female partners lovingly waiting back at home, and therefore had no aspirations to be involved in some sort of vaguely homosexual experience in a hotel in the middle of northern France, and for that matter were slightly offended by the idea of being allocated the room in question. After we had very carefully taken it in turns to shower and get dressed while the other stared at the nearby hedge outside the window, we were ready for dinner and as per usual I was feeling very hungry. Locking our room we walked back to the lift and took it back down to the reception area. Stepping from the lift we saw that the seating area in the middle of the lobby was filled with the other cyclists from our route staying there. After grabbing drinks from a selection laid out for us on the bar, we took seats and joined the group, being quickly introduced to the topics of conversation. One topic was everyone's experiences and opinions of their rooms as it turned out our embarrassing glass en suite was not only the standard fitment in the hotel but was also much less embarrassing than what some others had, where their en suite was in fact a complete glass rectangular cube in the centre of the room which had to be physically walked around to be able to traverse from one side of the room to the other. On a less disturbing sort of note there was a lot of discussion about how everyone was feeling, knowing that the finish line was less than twenty four hours away and that our little adventure into the heart of France was soon going to be over. As the hubbub of general chatter gently continued, a member of the support staff rose to his feet and began taking a register. Once satisfied that we were all present and accounted for, they announced that we were all to drink up as we were about to leave en route to our dinner reservation for the evening. Walking back across the car park we shortly came to a restaurant sitting in the middle of the retail park car park like an oversized version of a drive thru diner, as seen in many American films or shows. As we approached we were informed that it was part of a chain that had connections with one of the French breweries as this was the area known nationally more for its beer than its wine. Glancing quickly through the brown tinted windows the place looked to be popular as most tables looked full with lots of what looked like families eating together. Following the support staff we slowly shuffled in two by two through the door and were shown up stairs to a mezzanine floor which had three or four long ten -seater wooden tables which had been reserved for us. Sitting at the first seat available to me I found myself sitting next to the Kiwi fella whom I had spoken to in the courtyard of the last hotel some eleven hours previous. Harshal ended up sitting across the table from me as the rest of the seats slowly filled with other members of the group at large. As we settled down and began to chat, the waitresses came and took drinks orders. Looking around I gently relaxed into our tables' conversation which was concerned with the final finish line in the centre of Paris and who would be there to meet us when we made it there. It was at this point that I started to feel a little saddened and low by the fact that everyone else was going to be met at the finish by their wives, girlfriends or family, whereas I was not going to be greeted by such a sight; Rosie would be at work and within my family my brother and I were the only ones with valid passports meaning that one of the greatest successes of my life up to that point would pass unwitnessed by the people I cared about the most. This low feeling passed quickly as I snapped back to my natural positive state with the remembrance that this whole journey and in fact the year that had led up to it had been about personal growth, and so did not require validation from the outside world to justify it. Coming back to my philosophy of "it's not what you do, it's what it does to you that counts" in between the courses of food that evening our support staff informed us of the running order for the following day's cycle; they also informed us of the rough distances already conquered and reminded us of the charity's work that we were helping to contribute to. Towards the end of the dinner the support staff broached the subject of what everyone was planning on wearing to cycle in. Most people had already purchased the official logoed blue and white jersey of the ride; some had even gone to the point of buying the matching cycling shorts. Having nothing appropriate and clean to wear other than an old and skin-tight plain white t-shirt I felt the need to conform with the majority of my peers and purchased the official top. Before we all headed back to the hotel for the evening, I contemplated buying the matching shorts but refrained from doing so, being unsure as to how much money I would require for our day in Paris plus the return trip home. As we crossed the car park once again we all noticed movement coming from one of the third floor windows; as we got closer it turned out that Tony, the guy who had been wearing the Lucky Saddles cycling bibs, had actually only brought two with him, alternating between them every other day and washing them in the bath of his hotel room each evening, hanging them from the window overnight to dry in the cool night air ready for the following day's ride. This was extreme minimalist packing that I certainly saw logic to. However for hygiene reasons I could not imagine undertaking this myself. A few giggles were had by everyone at the massive variety of different luggage we had individually decided we would require, from the minimal extreme to the massively over encumbered. Months before departing we had been given a recommended equipment list. This simple list had been interpreted in a great number of individual ways. Feeling quite tired, but yet excited for the spectacle of the following day, most of us returned to our rooms to get ready for some sleep. Crashing in through the door of our room we remembered our earlier issues and so quickly I stood staring out of the window while Harshal used the toilet and got ready for bed. When it was my turn to use the strange glass wet room I was in and out in record time which for me was quite shocking as I can often spend quite lengthy periods of time sitting on the throne, as it is called. Climbing into bed, my last thoughts were of Rosie and as I lay there in the comfort and stillness I once again messaged her to say how I felt about her before pleasantly drifting off to a restful night's sleep, to recharge and repair my body ready for the final triumphant day of cycling madness on our way to Paris.

Chapter Twenty-One
Day Four: Compiègne to Paris

That morning I woke very early with a level of excitement so huge I almost fell out of bed. Directly rivalling the morning of my graduation, my anticipation for the challenge and personal glory ahead was mind blowing. The cycle rides to Bideford or Exeter were finally going to amount to something larger. Due to the smallness of the hour I strained against myself, respectfully not wishing to disturb Harshal who was still fast asleep on the other side of the room. I remained there clock-watching until it came to a more acceptable time at which I carefully rolled out of bed, grabbed my clothing and began to use the bathroom for my morning ablutions. I quickly showered, counting gently from one to one hundred as I read something once that said it takes approximately ninety seconds for a power shower to cover the average human body with water, which has led me to a precisely regulated showering protocol of three minutes once temperature has stabilised. Moments later I was enthroned upon the toilet. As I sat there Harshal's alarm sounded and within moments he was awake in perfect time for me to emerge from the glass room fully dressed minus socks, and sporting my newly acquired official charity cycling top. After a brief conversation regarding how we both slept I reassumed my position of staring out of the window while Harshal used the bathroom for his morning hygiene rituals. A few moments later Harshal stepped out from the bathroom, dressed and ready for the next few minutes, which were spent frantically packing as we readied our luggage in preparation for leaving the strange room. Lastly I removed my flip flops, placing them back in to one of the small external compartments of my suitcase. I carefully stretched a tight pair of white and blue cycling socks over my size eleven feet, followed by cycling shoes. Locking our room behind us we made our way downstairs for our last breakfast before getting to Paris.

The reception area was packed with our cycling peers who were all enjoying their rather standard breakfast. We joined the masses and started the morning in what felt, by this point, the normal way - a couple of rounds of fruit juice, interspaced between pain au chocolate and, croissants with apricot jam. The general chatter was about how today's ride was meant to be a short, fast-paced sort of sprint finish compared to the previous few days, as the distance was significantly smaller, weighing in at roughly half that of the first day's ride. The object of the scheduling was to convene at a park in the inner suburbs of the city after lunchtime to regroup, ready to roll en masse with cyclists from the other routes which ran parallel to ours, triumphantly reaching the final finishing line under the Eiffel tower as one huge peloton of some five hundred plus riders. For this to work correctly, we would only be stopping once for a refreshment stop, in a tiny village just outside Paris called Parisis, near Paris Charles de Gaulle Airport. It wasn't long till breakfast was over and we were once again retrieving our bikes from their overnight resting spot. Mounting our mechanical steeds, Harshal and I glanced back in through the doors of the hotel and waved as we pushed off. Riding along the exit slip road out of the retail park we crossed a road bridge over a busy highway which headed for Paris.

Soon we were cruising at a comfortable speed, making good progress as the road was smooth and flat. The ride was very enjoyable in the mid-morning air of gentle cooling breezes. Our conversation was light and friendly, often reflecting on our shared experiences of the previous days; the chips in Calais, the sneaky extra meal in Arras, and the dodgy transparent shower room of the night before all randomly dropped in and out of the conversation, as did our intrigue over how Abrar and Ajay's hotels compared. That morning we cycled through a forest which seemed to have had a network of several roundabouts, each with multiple tree lined avenues branching off in all directions. While traversing one of these roundabouts I spied signs directing to some castle or stately home which again made me think of Rosie and how I loved taking her on trips to historical places such as that. I remembered quite vividly a weekend down in Cornwall visiting first the Eden Project followed by the Lost Gardens of Heligan, and another such weekend spent visiting St Ives and Land's End. I added a cycling holiday through northern France to the list of our romantic trips to come. Soon we came round a corner and down a slight slope along the edge of the forest where we passed a small industrial park with a large saw mill and timber yard. Pressing on, we caught sight of more cyclists up ahead as we began to hear the sounds of aeroplanes heading to or from Paris Charles de Gaulle Airport a few miles away. A little further and we came alongside a very tall metal security fence which I assumed marked the boundary of the airport grounds as we could now make out the sights and sounds of the aircraft coming in to land. Seeing one of the route markers we turned off the road we had been on and headed towards what looked to be a small collection of beautiful little houses set down into the hillside; this turned quickly in to a tiny little village named Parisis; the houses were beautiful period buildings which looked possibly two hundred years old by my best guess. The streets were rough cobbles with sizable gaps between some of the stones, probably caused by many decades of wear having chipped away at them, and had unevenly rounded off the corners of adjacent looking stones. The kerbstones and pavements were huge pieces of rock, no doubt to help facilitate the dismount from some Shire horse or drawn carriage. The large, narrow tyres of my racing bike were designed for high speed over a smooth flat surface, not this irregularity giving me a great deal of difficulty that morning. I needed to perform a delicate balancing act involving constant minute changes to my body position and therefore the bike's centre of gravity, in order to remain in control of the steering and direction the bike was heading in, as not to get stuck in a rut. This was countered with the need to maintain a certain speed to remain on schedule that morning and reach the check points on time.

The slightly wider tyres of Harshal's mountain bike graced him with a wider more stable platform for him to traverse the cobbles and so he found this section of the morning's ride far easier. As we passed through the village we came around a corner to find one of the other cyclists from our route had fallen foul of the cobbles in more of an extreme manner than I had, getting stuck in a rut and which concluded in the bike ending up on top of him in a big tangled mess in the middle of the road. This was partly due to him being unable to unhook his cleated cycling shoes from the pedals in time to put a foot down and steady himself when the bike first began to go a bit wayward. This was an issue I was glad I did not have to deal with, as my cheap old trainers I cycled in allowed my feet complete freedom of movement whenever I felt the bike slip on the uneven ground. Once we had helped our peer get back on his way we followed behind until the road surface become a little more comfortable, at which point we soon found we were unable to maintain the base rate that he was comfortable cycling at; Harshal and I were alone together for a few mere moments before we were delighted to catch up with Abrar and Ajay for the first time that day. The four of us passed by a bakery and a corner café followed by a community building such as school hall or something similar, directly after which we spied the flags and the van which marked out our water/ lunch stop, which was set up in a coach park across the road from an open community park or green. On the grass of the park another couple of flags were set up, which was the designated rest point for cyclist from a different charity who had been shadowing our route and occasionally crossing paths with us since boarding the same ferry at Dover a couple of days previous. We had all commented how the other group had looked a far more ramshackle disorganised outfit compared to us. As in the vast majority of cases we had synchronised with each other wearing the official jersey of the ride ready for the finishing line. As we pulled up to a stop near a rank of cars we were greeted by the support crew and our fellow cyclists, most of whom were sitting down or laid out on the little grass strip which bordered part of the car park. After signing in we refilled our bottles and picked up a few snacks before sitting on the ground in as comfortable a spot as could be found. While lying out on the ground I noticed Lucky Saddles man who was fast asleep, lying across two commercial wheelie bins that were chained up under a tree at the back of the adjacent building. I zoned in and out of the various conversations going on around me, dropping in anecdotes and opinions in a laid back, devil-may -care-fashion.

This sort of midday refrain from activity was, however, short-lived, and soon we were readying ourselves to push off, back on to the road. As we left the water stop, initially heading back in a similar direction to that which we had come from, I quickly began to notice the terrain we were cycling through had become more of a suburban setting, with modern architecture and tarmacked smooth roads filled with countless cars parked seemingly everywhere, and frantic lines of traffic crossing each other at each intersection. Due to the fast paced and chaotic nature of the traffic we were forced to abandon our comfortable group cycling format in preference for single file dodging and weaving through gaps. At this point I noticed signage to say that we were not far from St Denis, the part of the city of Paris where the Moulin Rouge can be found. As we cycled on, the skies grew progressively darker and the air cooler, and the more urban and built up the landscape became. By the time the clouds burst and began depositing a short lived but heavy bout of rainfall down on us, we had reached a slightly dirty looking area which reminded me of Stokes Croft in Bristol. It was at this point that the speed at which the priority flow of traffic at an intersection was travelling was so great that our group got cut up further and I found myself tired, completely wet through, and cycling alone for the first time in nearly four days. This situation saddened me slightly, putting a bit of an uncomfortable spin on the experience of cycling through what seemed to be the hard working, deprived commercial shell which encased and surrounded the more beautiful and world famous centre of the city of Paris. Thankfully this unpleasant damping of both my clothes and my spirits was only short lived, and as the weather brightened, so did my positive silver lining nature, shining through and removing any presence of a cloud from my outlook. Feeling positive and peaceful once again I got back to paying more attention to my surroundings and the ramshackle beauty of the area, which seemed to get older and more historically beautiful with every turn of the pedals, signifying that I was getting further and further in towards the centre of Paris. I even found myself cycling along with a couple of other riders, and that Harshal was within sight a little further up the road. I thought of Rosie and wondered what she would have been doing at that precise moment, coming to the conclusion that she would possibly be at work and therefore unable to answer, so I resisted the temptation to add to my phone bill by phoning her. It turned out that we were actually coming very close to the rally point where our route number three intersected and joined two others, routes one and four I believe, so that we could cycle together towards the final finishing line. Before getting to the finishing line, we would be joined by routes two and five, who had also converged together at an alternative rally point. The architecture and atmosphere had by this point become quite bohemian and artisan, reminding me of some of the streets Rosie and I walked down when we came to Paris for a romantic weekend a few months earlier in late January of that year. The road swept around a long left hand bend to reveal the spectacular entrance to one of the many beautiful parks in the city of Paris, the sight of which conjured up images of Vassals Park in Bristol and Victoria Park in the city of Bath, two places that my family and I spent a considerably large amount of time during my childhood. Through the seemingly ancient wrought iron gates I could see dozens of bikes parked up resting by the gates and fences, and I could see Abrar and Ajay amongst the crowd that was gathered just inside. We had arrived at the rally point. Scooting my bike to a stop just outside I forcefully pushed the gates open causing a load of clattering which signalled my arrival, which was met with happy greetings and smiles from all around. Once I was officially signed in I decided that first port of call was to use the lavatory which was to be found up a couple of steps to me in a small but beautiful white stone semi-circular building to the right of the park entrance. Having relieved myself I began to mingle amongst the crowd of cyclists; some faces I knew, others I didn't, and so proceeded to enquire which route they had been part of and how they had found the whole experience. As the sun was shining the park looked a beautiful summery location; some of the cyclists had even decided to partake in an ice-cream from a little octagonal wooden hut a few paces further into the park near to what looked to be a picnic area. Harshal, Ajay and Abrar were standing by a little metal railing over in the direction of the hut so I wandered over, with every step debating the pros and cons of buying an ice-cream myself. As if by magic the moment after deciding I did not require the frozen dairy product an announcement was made by the support staff that we were on schedule but only just barely and that we were needed to return to our bikes and assemble on the pavement outside the entrance of the park, where we were to receive further instructions regarding a couple of little surprises that were in store for us during the final assault on the finish line, which was to be near as makes no difference under the Eiffel Tower. With this as confirmation that I didn't want or have time for an ice-cream I turned 180 degrees and joined the march of cyclists eager to get back on two wheels.

With my bike back between my legs and two of us, man and machine, leaning gently against a wall, I listened and watched as the support van that had been parked on the pavement next to the entrance of the park gently trundled off back on to the road surface, before the gentleman hanging out the back door with a megaphone in his hand explained that due in part to the size of the cycling group as a whole - some five hundred odd two wheeled nutters like me The Gendarmerie, the Parisian police, had agreed to help support our final leg by temporarily closing certain roads and would act as outriders, escorting us through the streets down to our final destination at the heart of this beautiful and world famous city. This included the chance of a lifetime opportunity to stop for a photograph of the entire group circling the Arc de Triomphe, which on any other day would be an impossible feat due to the location being one of the busiest, chaotic and most dangerous roundabouts in the world.

Two at a time we were shepherded off the pavement and down the road slowly, we all initially found it difficult to maintain a gentle pace, due the pent up excitement of the occasion. But once the nervous excitement had mellowed slightly with the steady rhythm of our pedalling, I began to notice that the pavements of the tree lined streets we were travelling were filed with smiling faces and cheering voices of the city's inhabitants celebrating us and cheering us on as if we were the Tour de France professionals, proving to me that it wasn't just the countryside townspeople of the little villages and hamlets, but the French as a nation who enjoyed the spectacle of a group of random cyclists riding past their front door. It was magical. The support of the crowd helped me ignore the fact that the deeper in to the centre we got, the more cobblestoned the road surface got, although these stones were far smoother and more rounded off than the ones we had experienced coming through Parisis. That said, a couple of the riders a little way in front of me did suffer coming off of their bikes and in one such case causing a pile-up which brought our slow steady pace to a standstill momentarily.

Once everyone was safely moving again it wasn't long till we could see the Arc de Triomphe roundabout. As we emerged, the roundabout was uncharacteristically silent, filled with hundreds of anticipant cyclists remaking the normal six lanes of uncontrolled unregulated traffic mayhem. The weather by this point was truly glorious, bright and sunny with a cool breeze calmly blowing through the occasional trees which surround the roundabout at the mouth of the various roads which enter on to it. This remained so while all five hundred of us took photos of ourselves and our cycling friends to help immortalise the memory in our minds. There was not a cloud in the sky for a good five or six minutes, right up until the announcement was made that preparations were in order for official publicity photos to be made of the five hundred strong group as a whole by a professional photographer; this then became a race against the weather as clouds started rolling in from all directions. With merely seconds to spare before the sun slipped behind a mild grey cloud the shot was taken and we were once again given the all clear to leave the area, shepherded once again by the support team and the Gendarmerie towards our finish line, the giant looming presence of the Eiffel Tower now barely more than a couple of streets away.

Within a couple of short minutes I found myself in sight of the base of the tower and jetties from where you can catch one of the city's sightseeing river boat cruises like the one I took with Rosie a few months previous. As we cycled across a bridge on to Île-de-France, the massive river island that is at the very heart of the centre of Paris, I came directly in shot of a photographer who was crouched in the middle of the road getting action shots of cyclists as we gently glided past only a few inches from the end of his lens on the final ten metre assault of a life affirming three hundred plus mile journey from the capital of one great nation to the capital of its neighbour.

As I became the focus of the photographer's camera I adjusted my pose and threw my black gloved left fist up and punched the air trying to look as dramatic as one can when half knackered sitting on a push bike in blue and white Lycra. I quickly realised that I was actually heading straight for the poor cameraman and hastily banked left unknowingly allowing for one of the greatest and most treasured photographs of me ever to be taken, which was blown up into an A3 size piece of box art by my friends at Ilfracombe photo shop upon my return to England, and has ever since hung proudly on the wall in the living room of my flat. Just past the photographer came the flags which signalled the official finish line and the triumphant completion of the ride. Throwing in a little bit of drift racing style that my RX-8 would have approved of I skidded over the line. I slid to a stop, carefully balanced as not to fall over and end up with the bike on my shoulders; this I have to admit was possibly more luck than judgement but on all accounts looked as spectacularly skilful as I had hoped for. Stepping down off the bike and pulling it next to me I took a couple of paces forward towards the designated sign-in area for riders from route three joining the crowd of smiling, happy and exhausted faces I had come to recognise over the previous four days. Once I had signed in, I was presented with my medal which reads:

'Exhaustion to elation,

Ride L2P

500 riders, 5 routes, 1 goal

July 2011'

This medal hangs from one of my bookcases in the flat's dining area and is the another visual reminder of that day and the pride I felt having completed the journey, almost like graduating all over again except for one depressing fact which made me feel quite sad and disappointed for a brief moment. As I looked around, most of my cycling peers were standing with and introducing each other to their families and loved ones, who had all made the journey from Great Britain or even further afield to be there waiting on the finish line to give them a heroes' welcome and celebrate the victory with them. Whereas I had no one; neither of my parents had passports, my brother was busy with his own life and family unit, and my dearest Rosie had not been able to take time off of work. For the first time in his history a man of a close knit family and thousands of friends felt alone; it was a feeling I did not find pleasant. Fortunately my moment of despair was broken as quickly as it had begun by the uplifting presence of Harshal, Abrar, and Ajay who had decided that the four of us would follow the developing trend of the other cycling partnerships and have a series of photos taken standing together side by side with the Eiffel Tower looking magnificent in the background of the shot. This quickly turned into some sort of catalogue photo shoot with us having to take multiple frames, some with our sunglasses on, others without, some with our bikes in front of us, to the side of us and even a couple with our bikes lifted high above our heads like trophies. Eventually we came to take the photo that sits on the windowsill in my dining area. The journey was over, or so we thought, but the fun was just beginning. The support staff made another announcement which was that now we had reached the finish line for the journey to Paris we had to split back in to our five route travelling groups, get back on our bikes and follow our respective members of staff to our hotels and get checked in for the event of getting ready for the celebratory final diners which were being held in our honour that evening, and that during dinner we would be given our travel arrangements for the journey back to London the following evening. With that, we one by one got back in the saddle and joined the route three formation heading for our hotel; the first hotel of the trip large enough to house all the one hundred and twenty riders from route three together, the hotel in question turned out to be another fairly mediocre budget Ibis, only this time the Ibis Eiffel which is not as close to the tower as its name would suggest, it is still in sight of it, but then a good half of the city is due to the sky scraping size and solitude of the Eiffel Tower. Once again we took to the streets only this time more tired, missing the police escort and the relative safety of a five hundred strong pack. We backtracked slightly before turning in a new direction, and made our way silently down some quite peaceful roads until we reached our hotel in a very casual understated manner. This was where we parted company with our steeds as we no longer had requirement for them before we returned to home soil. The bikes were also being segregated into three lots; the first was for the people who needed to return to the start line at the aerodrome hotel Croydon to pick up their car, which was being held in the hotel car park, and the second group was for individuals such as me who were happy to collect their bikes upon our arrival at St Pancras train station, the terminal stop for our Eurostar and the official end of our homeward journey. The third option was for riders taking on additional challenges straight off the back of the L2P, such as the Paris to Geneva or those who planned to stay in France for more relaxed reasons. My bike however did cause additional confusion as the borrowed wheels had to be returned and exchanged for my problematic originals. Before this occurred, I quickly made a mental note of the tyre brand with the intention of purchasing a pair as soon as I was back home typing away at my computer once again. Stepping in through the front door of the Ibis it looked far larger, and a little more expensive than the one we had stayed in back in Arras; I later found out that it had over five hundred rooms. Standing by the reception desk was the now all too well recognised A-frame notice board explaining that dinner this evening was going to be being held at the Novotel a little way across town and that transport had been laid on in the form of a couple of coaches that would be collecting us for dinner at exactly seven o'clock outside the front of the Ibis. Harshal and I were eager to get to our room to rest a little before getting suited and booted ready for our dinner. Entering our room for the first time we quickly came to the realisation that it was an enlarged mirror image of our room in the Ibis of Arras. The furniture and fittings were identical, as was the rough painted woodchip wall paper and the room's colour scheme, as if to say that both hotels were furnished with items from a single job lot. This may have been to maintain brand standardisation. The only noticeable difference between the rooms was that the room in Paris was approximately ten percent larger in footprint, making it on par with the room in Calais as the most spacious of our trip. Laying our luggage on the floor at the foot of our beds we lay back and switched on the news to get caught up on world events which seemed even more distant and alien to us than ever before. For the next forty minutes we both took a power nap to recharge and reset. When we awoke we performed our usual routine, deciding who was going to use the bathroom first; in this case it was Harshal and so as he showered I checked my email and sent Rosie my customary messages and informed her that although I was enjoying my adventure I couldn't wait to be back home in my little ground floor flat tucked away in a sleepy little English seaside town, and be able to hold her again. During our short conversation it came to my attention that due to the lateness of the hour that we would return to London I was going to be left with the dilemma of having to find overnight accommodation for me and my bike before I could travel back to my home county; this was something I had not planned for. Worrying for my safety and comfort far more than I did, and being a pedantically over-organised individual, Rosie sprang in to action and made arrangements for her sister Bonnie who lived with her husband to be in south London, to pick me up from the train station when the Eurostar arrived and give me a bed for the evening. This was a most humbling offer that I gladly accepted. The alternatives, although numerous, were for the most part far less comforting and in some cases quite costly which given the date and the advanced nature of the month I was not as flushed with funds as I would have chosen to be when faced with such an approaching dilemma. Harshal emerged from the bathroom at precisely the moment my conversation with Rosie had ended. He was looking sharp in a sort of "I'm bold but working it" style, wearing a white shirt that had the arms turned up, with black suit trousers plus a stylish sleeveless black pullover. He was now patiently waiting for me to begin my own grooming procedure. Laying my phone down, I took to the bathroom and commenced my showering. Some ten minutes later we were both ready for dinner looking like extras from the music video for one of my favourite ZZ Top songs, 'Sharp Dressed Man'. Leaving our room and returning to the reception we were greeted by the sight of all the other riders, some fully suited, some rocking a more smart casual kind of attire. Steadily we were herded on to a couple of coaches which pulled up outside before the short drive over to the Novotel which, given the tiny distance, seemed to take ages due to the volume of traffic that the coaches had to navigate through. Eventually we arrived at the Novotel, turning off of the main road in to the undercover vehicle entrance. We disembarked and made our way inside the tall glass building and were ushered up an escalator to what I think may have been the reception and public bar. The whole place had a light shiny elegance to it that seemed to suggest this was a higher class of establishment than the one we were spending the night in. Being that I had become quite a connoisseur and a lover of fancy yet affordable hotels and restaurants, where the bill may not be tiny, the attention to customer service and quality of the facilities give you a reassuring feeling of value for money. I began to feel more comfortable and that I was appropriately dressed, standing there in one of my pinstriped grey Daniel Graham suits as the hotel bar staff waltzed around us handing out welcome drinks. Once we had all been given a flute of champagne or orange juice alternative for the non-drinking contingent amongst us we were again shepherded, this time in to the dining room. The double doors opened to reveal a large space, capable of seating the three hundred odd riders who had congregated with us at the inner city park earlier that day. Elegantly minimal in its styling, the room was filled with a great rank of ten seater rectangular tables stretching back from one end of the room to the other, bordered each side by round tables which were positioned close to the walls. The colour scheme of the room was a pale coffee colour to the lower half of the walls, which stopped just below the line of wall hanging head height lighting, and gave away to a classy cream colour which capped the room. The double doors, which could be found at the corners of the room, acted as both exits and entrances to side rooms. Periodically down the length of the room large columns could be seen. These columns stretched from floor to ceiling and were monotone, painted in the coffee colour. Close to these columns were wall-mounted TV screens allowing for those seated facing the back of the room to comfortably see the events occurring on the stage and main projector screen situated at the front of the room without the risk of neck injury. The tables were a mix of two styles depending on their position within the room, with the ones to the centre of the room predominantly being glass topped and with the others being covered in a white tablecloth. All were seated with middle backed chairs with deep red cushions. The density of the furniture layout gave little opportunity to assess the style of the carpet which was underfoot. The four of us, Harshal Ajay, Abrar and I, took our seats in a group at one end of a long table roughly central to the hall. With me sitting at the head flanked to the left by Abrar and the right by Harshal followed by Ajay, we were joined by a random mixture of cyclists who recognised us and filled the rest of the seats at our table. The evening began with presentations and video messages from the charity staff and from some of the patients and families that had benefited from work funded by the charity and ultimately by the hard work of those of us who took up the challenge. There were announcements regarding the total raised so far thanks to our efforts. Special mentions were made for a number of specific riders, one of whom had cycled down from Manchester to London as an extreme warm up to his London to Paris journey, a female rider who had the misfortune of more tyre changes then even I had endured, and another female rider who had raised more money in her pre-challenge sponsorship campaign than three of her peers combined. After the presentations a camera roll of all the official photos taken of routes one, thee, and four over the past three hundred odd miles was slowly displayed on the screens around the room. As the camera roll proceeded a call was given to say that our food was ready. Table by table we ventured into the side rooms to find long tables and hot plates of food, each served to us carvery style by members of the hotel's waiting staff. Over the course of the next hour or so I made several trips with the intention of trying a little of everything, and a bit more of that I found most pleasant. The conversation at our table was mainly a light mix of recollections and opinions looking back over the previous few days or even longer. This was coupled with the telling of jokes, or characterful stories of each individual's lives. We also discussed who would be interested in one of the longer challenges such as London to Paris then on to Geneva, or potentially Land's End to John O'Groats if anyone wished to remain domestic in the future.

At the end of our dinner the announcement was made that those who wished to get an early night with the intention to be up bright and early to secure a good spot to watch the Tour de France professionals come in, there would be coaches leaving imminently. For those who remained, the well-deserved night in Paris was ours for the taking to celebrate with how ever we wished. This would however require us being able to make our own way back to our hotels. At this point I had indulged in several glasses of French wine and was not prepared to call it quits yet. It was at this point that Abrar and Ajay made arrangements to go back to the hotel wanting a restful night's sleep, Harshal and I hung around the Novotel bar long enough to make friends with a couple of other cyclists who wanted to see a little more of the Parisian night life but were worried about getting back to the Ibis later on. With calm confidence I assured our new friends that not only did I have the step by step journey back there laid out in my mind as I had taken mental note of road names and landmarks on the coach journey over, but I also had no intentions of getting so blind drunk that I would lose said map, furthermore I had no desire to be out till sun rise, believing that approximately 1 to 1:30 a.m. was sufficient a time to get to bed. We decided that we would return to the area around the Ibis, having noticed a couple of nice looking little bars in the vicinity. Leaving the Novotel minutes after the last bus we flagged down a taxi, being the man with the map in his head I was the main one to converse with the cab driver as to our destination. He replied that he did not know the hotel but he knew the street name where I said it was located and agreed with the route that I had suggested, commenting that he felt it was mad for the hotel to be named after the Eiffel Tower when it was in a different sector of the city to its namesake landmark.

Pulling up beside bar a couple of streets away from the Ibis, we thanked and paid our driver before entering. The wooden canopied patio out the front of the bar was filled with a couple of tables of cyclists who had returned to the hotel on the coach only to realise how early it was and decide one more drink wouldn't hurt. One of these was Mr Lucky Saddles; once we had been to the bar and purchased drinks we stepped out on to the patio and joined the flock. Upon my arrival cheers and calls were raised: "Here comes the pannierman come to join us" and other such lines revolving around my recently acquired nickname. Receiving my greetings with a smile and a swing of my drink I sat down and become involved with the conversation. The topics and flow of conversation echoed that of the dinner table earlier in the evening, only this time with a different mix of people. A while passed swiftly with gentle conversation until Tony the Lucky Saddles man announced:

"Here she comes again, lads." The 'she' that he was referring to was a young barmaid who was rounding up finished glasses for the dish washer. At a guess I would say she was approximately twenty one years of age, and was blessed with very pretty facial features, similar to a dark eyed brunette version of my partner Rosie. The general consensus around the table was that she was indeed attractive; however from my own opinion she lacked a certain amount of the feminine curves that I look for in a woman. As our barmaid dutifully cleared our tables, she tried to explain that we were fast approaching closing time. Upon the receipt of this information Tony boldly set about cheekily attempting to flirt with her using an incomprehensible combination of incredibly badly pronounced and in some cases flat out incorrect French terms, English, and what I can only assume was his own spontaneously generated language that only he could decrypt. This was all topped off with a terribly over the top attempt at a French accent, reminiscent of the policeman character in the British sitcom *'Allo 'Allo!* This hilariously cringeworthy spectacle was performed to convince her to keep the bar open for us to continue drinking. This was completely unsuccessful and soon we were all left in search of the next drinking establishment. At this point Harshal decided that he was tired and wished to return to the Ibis and was fully capable of doing so alone if I felt I wished to continue the evening. Promising to be as silent as possible when I returned, I bid him goodnight and set off to continue drinking with the group which included the Bentley boys. Walking a couple more streets away we eventually found another delightful looking café/bar with another chic outside seating area for us to take over and share a few more beverages. Our conversation had turned in to more of a question and answer session enquiring as to the reasoning for the Bentley boys' connection to and love for the brand. I listened carefully and slowly I learned how they were all work colleagues and/or family who centred on the patriarchal figure who was the manager of the high end Bentley franchise car dealership they all worked for. The youngest of the group was not only one of the mechanics, but also was his son, and so when they decided to undertake the London to Paris they enlisted team mates from amongst the rest of the staff and acquired branded team cycling gear, luggage and smart casual clothing through the company as a form of advertising which had clearly been successful at least in the eyes of this Bristolian microbiology graduate. As the evening rolled on and became the midnight hour, this next bar began to shut up shop for the night. At this point the youngest of the Bentley boys, whom I believe may have been called Paul although my memory is somewhat hazy on this point, announces that while looking for another bar in walking distance his mobile phone application may have suggested a brothel. Glancing at the screen I informed him that he was probably correct in his assumption as the address given for the establishment was over the other side of the city centre in the area around the Moulin Rouge. This was a somewhat dodgy area, known for casual street crime late at night. It was also quite a hike from our current location. Deciding we were better off exploring the area around our hotel further we hit the street in search of some sort of respectable midnight entertainment; after searching for a short while we came across a deposit rack for the Parisian equivalent of the London public cycle hire scheme often referred to as Boris Bikes after the city's Mayor Boris Johnson, who pioneered the idea and set up the London scheme. For a good five possibly ten minutes we stood there and contemplated the hilariously bonkers idea that for no reason at all other than having nothing else to do, ten English gentlemen hire push bikes and

171

cycle in big circuits round the streets of Paris at 12:30 a.m. at night, pissed up and exhausted after cycling over three hundred miles to get there on bikes which they already owned. What's worse is that in the midnight madness we all agreed that this logically backwards and insanely pointless plan was somehow a good idea that was to be carried out with most haste. It got as far as only being abandoned once we were informed by the payment terminal that the deposit that would be taken from our debit cards would be in the region of two thousand pounds each. This was due to the fact we were neither Paris residents nor French nationals. Sulking away like little children who had been denied the fashionable gift at Christmas, on through the late night streets we walked. We slowly returned to the Ibis, beginning to sober up. By the time we reached the hotel we had all decided that the eventful evening had reached its bizarre anti-climactic end. Bidding everyone a good night and pleasant sleep I made my way to my room opening the door as quietly as possible to not disturb Harshal, who it turned out was still awake due to the short amount of time that had actually passed between him returning and me getting back. At his request I gave him a brief summary of the events that transpired in his absence. Before we turned off our bedside lights and settled down into our beds for the last hotel sleep of the trip, I quickly checked my email and Facebook accounts in case of anything I may have missed; receiving nothing but junk mail I turned my phone to standby and plugged it in to its charger. Feeling anticipant about the sporting spectacle I was to observe the following day I fell fast asleep as soon as the room went dark.

Chapter Twenty-Two

Day Five: Paris, the Tour De France and Our Repatriation to England

Morning came blissfully bright and cheerful; with it my energy was renewed ready for the challenges, trials, sights, and sounds of the day ahead. As we lay there in our beds with bright sunlight streaming in through the window before being gently diffused into the room through the pale cream curtains, Harshal and I enjoyed a quiet little conversation regarding how lucky we both felt to have been placed together having originally signed up as individuals; we had gotten on well and become quite good friends. We had really helped each other enjoy the cycling experience; we also discussed how fortunate it was that we met Abrar and Ajay, both of whom had played major roles in the events of the previous days. Finally we both admitted that it felt strange that we were not rushing to slip in to our cycling shorts and furthermore that we wouldn't be spending the next eight hours sitting on a bike, and most of all that we were going to be home in approximately sixteen hours and may never see each other again. It was a very sombre shock back to reality that the journey that had both caused and defined our friendship was almost over. We agreed to make the most of our day together so that we should do all we could to enjoy it. We decided we would keep in contact so that if the opportunity were to arise we could cycle together again someday and that this networking would, at their discretion, include keeping in contact with Abrar and Ajay so the awesome foursome could be fully reunited in the future. As per our now well-rehearsed and standardised morning practice we took turns getting showered and dressed only this time the cycling attire was replaced by jeans and t-shirt or in my case board shorts with a t-shirt due to my partial beach bum lifestyle living near the coast in north Devon. Once fully dressed and packed we ventured downstairs for our buffet breakfast. This was a near carbon copy of the one we had partaken in Arras and generally followed the same theme of all the mornings of the previous days. The only difference was that it didn't terminate with the sight of our bikes. Instead we were informed we would not be depositing our luggage at reception to be collected by the support staff. The reason for this was the van, which was carrying our bikes back to home soil, had already departed and so we were left to make our own arrangements for our overnight bags. Some of our peers informed us that the Ibis had a locker room on the lower ground floor but this turned out to be full; it was also explained that as we were slightly later that normal Abrar and Ajay had already consumed their breakfast and departed from the hotel for the day planning to return to collect their bags from the locker room in the evening, taking a detour while on route to Gare du Nord, the Parisian Eurostar terminal and the beginning of our homeward journey. The fact the locker room was full left Harshal, me and a number of other riders with the inconvenience of having to carry our luggage round the city with us all day, even though we had agreed we would make use of the Metro, the Parisian equivalent of the London underground, which unlike its British counterpart spends a large percentage of its time above ground with some platforms being built several feet up in the air and some sections of track needing to cross bridges between Île-de-France and the city mainland. Composing ourselves we finished breakfast and told the last of our cycling peers we would see them that evening and departed the hotel, trundling our cases beside us. Our first plan was to make our way to a more tourist centred shopping area for some souvenirs to further weigh down our baggage; the first obstacle we had to negotiate was to cross the nearby main road in search of the local Metro station. On our way there we passed the first of the drinking venues of the evening before. In the daylight, it looked just as comfortable and relaxed an atmosphere as it had done some ten hours previous, only far busier with the patio tables filled by people enjoying a French café and a crepe in the warm mid-morning air. It was a delightful scene that played too many of the international stereotypes about the chic and stylish side of French culture. Getting to our station we purchased tickets and made our way to the platform to await the next trains which, like the circle line of the London underground, were scheduled only a few minutes apart. Boarding the train with our luggage we quickly found our bag to be an awkward encumbrance, not heavy but an annoying presence. We made our way round the city to the Champs-Élysées and found that it was quiet but already slowly beginning to fill as the city prepared for the final stage of the Tour de France to roll in which was still some hours away at the time. After walking around the immediate area for a little while still feeling burdened by our bags we bumped in to some cyclist who informed us that they had previously been suffering in a similar manner and had solved the situation by use of the locker room at the Gare du Nord station. Deciding that we had a fairly large amount of the day still to fill before the pro's cycled in we ventured back to the Metro and made our way to the Gare du Nord, planning to deposit our bags and collect them in the evening before boarding the Eurostar, thus lightening our load and allowing us to enjoy the atmosphere of the event more easily. During the journey I was able to get in contact with Abrar, who along with Ajay was on

175

his way to Concorde, another area of the city I had previously visited with Rosie while visiting the Louvre during our romantic weekend sightseeing in the city. We explained our current movements and agreed that once bagless, Harshal and I would make haste over to their location and reunite with them, ready to find an optimum view point for the four of us to watch the race. Once across town and inside the station Harshal and I were confronted with yet more complications to our recreation, the first being that as we arrived in the historic train terminal we had to fight our way through a seemingly endless and massive crowd of people leaving the station having recently disembarked trains that ferried them in from all corners of the globe to be part of and witness the day's sporting event. Being that I was physically the larger and heavier of the two of us I was chosen to spearhead our charge through the masses, making a brief gap for Harshal to follow me through. Eventually we made it through to find that under the overhead sign for the luggage store was a wide metal staircase which led down to a basement area. To our disappointment the staircase was filled with an enormous queue of people snaking left to right as it backed up the stairs; these were mainly other cyclists wishing to do as we had planned to and make use of the station's storage facility for the day. Joining the back of the queue in a very ordered polite manner we began waiting for it to move. After some ten minutes had passed and no movement was made of the line we started to worry that we could waste the day in a futile and ironic attempt not to waste the day. Moments later we witnessed a couple of cyclists whom we recognised from our route carrying their luggage back up from the basement storage area; they came over to us and explained that the luggage room was basically already full up and that they had been turned away. Harshal looked devastated by this news and I too felt my eternal optimism was on shaky ground with the reality of the situation but I held my nerve and attempted to formulate an alternate solution. As we discussed the dilemma we recalled walking past a Mercure hotel just across

176

the road from the station. Deciding to chance it we left the Gare du Nord and made our way through the crowd as a group. Upon arriving at the Mercure moments later we defined which one of our small group had the best command on the French language and therefore would be most suitable to respectfully request the storage of our belongings by the hotel's staff. The concierge was a most helpful individual who kindly listened to our plight and graciously agreed to our request explaining that this was not the first occasion the dilemma had occurred, informing us that there was a small fee for the service as we were not guests of the hotel; this turned out to be such a small and insignificant amount of money that we gladly accepted the terms. He pointed us in the direction of a very grand wooden staircase; this rose from the ground up through the hotel floors in the middle of the left hand wall of the hotel lobby as we stood looking at the reception desk. To one side of the staircase was a small wooden door whose engravings matched that of the staircase banister rails. Standing in front of and slightly to one side of this door was a small podium or lectern. Grabbing a key, the concierge opened the door which revealed the hotel luggage room. Standing at the lectern one by one he asked us for our bags, each bag was given a yellow security tag around the handle and the corresponding numbered ticket handed to the bag's owner for identification upon collection later. Leaving the hotel bagless and feeling much lighter and much happier than we had arrived, our temporary group disbanded as we all our own plans for the day. Contacting Abrar and Ajay I informed them of the cause of our delay and the steps we had been required to take to remedy the situation, and that we were en route to their location finally. Getting on the Metro once again we headed straight for Place de le Concorde.

Upon our arrival at our destination Harshal and I once again waded through the crowds till we found ourselves at the entrance to the park which leads on to the Louvre, pausing at the entrance we contacted Abrar and Ajay once again and waited for a while for them to rendezvous with us. Taking a slow and gentle stroll around the park together the four of us discussed a huge range of topics covering every aspect of modern life from banking, business and global finance through to healthcare and lifestyle. Not forgetting culture, travel, and how sport and food linked in to all such topics as a fully integrated web of the modern world. We stopped for a coffee at a little bohemian café we stumbled on near the centre of the park. Not being a fan of coffee I instead opted for a glass of water. We chose to sit outside in the warm midday air, sitting on the café's white metal garden furniture underneath the delicate shade of the well maintained tree line nearby. Time passed steadily as we sat still discussing the world till Ajay suggested that we begin finding our way to a vantage point suitable for us to watch the afternoon's race. Agreeing that it was a sensible idea we called over a waitress and requested our bill. Walking back through the park we could see that the crowds were amassing, becoming denser and more entrenched with every moment. The realisation came that we may end up standing quite far back deep in the crowd, if we attempted to watch the event from one of the more popular areas of the route. As a return to our jovial form we began once again putting the world to rights as we searched the event route for an opening in the crowd which would allow us to stand against the roadside railings which mark the route and separate the legions of fans from their heroes. As we walked the concept of us staying in touch once again was raised as was the idea of undertaking another cycle ride together, maybe an even longer one and one with a more personal focus on the four of us. I believe it was Ajay who once again pointed out that one half of our cycling team was of Indian heritage and a quarter was of Pakistani ancestry, so why didn't we attempt to cycle for charity from London to Jaipur, capital of Rajasthan, a state of India which borders Pakistan? This region of the globe was of cultural significance to our whole cycling team either through bloodlines or in my case a love of exported cuisine. The idea of one day undertaking such a trip as the only domestically British and Caucasian member of an ethnically diverse sporting outfit appealed to the adventurous pioneering side of my nature. I would gladly accept the chance of the undertaking. Walking on we eventually found a spot by the river that was uncrowded allowing us to get right up to and rest against the railings only a couple of feet away from the tarmac of the road surface, which had seen the outriders and advance support crews who signal the arrival of the leading cyclists a substantial distance before they actually reach that location. Knowing that it would not be long till our area was equally swamped with people as where we had come from we decided to fortify our position as best as was possible only leaving one person at a time to find a toilet, and in my case a couple of times in search of food. As the professional equivalents of us began rolling in I noticed two facts, the first being that their ground covering speed was similar to that of car driving sedately through a small town centre. This was somewhere in the region of 30mph, a speed that I was able to attain on a bike but could only maintain for a few minutes of travel, not several complete back to back days on the road. As they passed us in a blaze of colour, the second fact I noticed was that they were followed swiftly by an immense cavalcade of support vehicles. It was an amazing spectacle. A beautiful warm summer's day with an atmosphere of friendship and communal enjoyment to rival that of a music festival. Except this wasn't a sixty acre field in the countryside county of rural Somerset, this was an entire capital city of a western country that had been brought to a standstill as hundreds of thousands of people from all across the globe crowded the streets to witness one of the greatest and most prestigious sporting events in the world occurring right in front of them. The beauty of the occasion and the fact that I had been able to share in it with three wonderful individuals humbled me, making me once again feel incredibly lucky and fortunate to be there. As the TDF continued to power though the streets in front of us, knocking down their laps of the final stage circuit,

I noted most of the riders were slight of frame and stature; I was later informed that the approximate average height and weight for a TDF rider is five feet ten inches tall and only 70 kg, or in other words eleven stones. These facts combined to mean that should I get my chance to be photographed with one of the TDF cycling elite, we would probably stand eye to eye. I would however look like some brutish feral, cave man by comparison being that I am five feet eleven inches and an average of 85kg or 13 stone six pounds, with a body fat percentage of 22%. Another difference that would be easily noticed would be that I allow myself to be as hairy as nature intended me to be. Pro cyclists are often waxed to remain hairless, streamlined and aerodynamic, characteristics that I ascribe more to the feminine half of our species. As the race concluded the crowd began to thin slightly as the majority of people made their way to their hotels or homes to prepare for celebrations or commiserations in honour of their chosen cyclist or cycling team. As we were not in sight of the final finish line on the Champs-Élysées or any of the run off area where riders dismounted their bikes to be met by their support staff and team management, we watched one of the many giant screens which televised the final moments of each rider's race and gave the final statistics and standings of the completion, such as the winners of the various stages, the overall winning team and the winning individual rider. Being a very patriotic British national it was a pleasant sight to see a fellow Brit and hero of mine the Manx missile, Mark Cavendish MBE representing his nation on the scoreboard by being the first Brit to win the points classification also known as the green jersey. With the race finally over we realised that our day together was almost over and that we were soon to start our journey home. As we walked slowly back towards the closest Metro station we began to see the massive crowds of people had not really thinned out much but had instead moved from being evenly spread out around the race route to now creating potentially dangerous sea of people moving like a tidal wave funnelling into the tiny channel that was the entrance to the Metro station. At this point it dawned upon us that we were caught in a minor paradoxical situation, not wanting to add to the chaos by joining the crowd, but having to make our way to the Gare du Nord in time to make our transport home and not get stranded in the middle of France with no accommodation. Other constrains on our need for cross town travel were as follows: if we were to make the Eurostar, would we also have the time to collect our bags from the Mercure or the Ibis (in the case of Abrar's luggage) or would some French hoteliers be acquiring new clothing at our expense? On top of this I began to feel hungry once again. We decided that splitting back into two pairs and reconvening at our destination was the best idea as we would stand a better chance of getting through to a Metro train as a pair than we would as a four piece. This also eliminated the requirement for Abrar and Ajay to accompany us to the Mercure or for Harshal and me to detour needlessly in completely the opposite direction to what we needed to travel, just so we could accompany Abrar and Ajay to the Ibis. At this point my knowledge and previous experience of walking round the streets of Paris with Rosie came a valuable asset as instead of joining the mob trying to cram in to the first Metro station we came to, I was able to navigate from memory round to another Metro station in the nearby area which had not been part of the TDF route and therefore was still busy but not to the same worrying extreme. We waited and queued on the platform for what felt like an age until we were among the next to be ushered aboard the following train. As it arrived I could see it was packed and as the doors opened only two people stepped off on to the platform and were replaced by six people boarding. These people included Harshal and me; much to my relief we were properly on our way bound for the Gare du Nord. It was hot sweaty, cramped and uncomfortable but we were making progress and travelling over and under the city streets at a quicker pace than we could have walked ourselves. Stopping at each station we could see the faces of all the people lined up along the platforms waiting to catch a train.

Some looked tired, some looked angry, but most were still upbeat and still in awe of the sporting spectacle we had all witnessed. At each station it was only an odd couple of individuals who actually got off the train and it always seemed to be that more got on than had alighted, making the train progressively more sweaty, cramped and uncomfortable although this could have been a biased observation that twisted my subjective view from within the affected frame. Eventually we arrived at our stop. As Harshal and I alighted from the train we found ourselves in a steady stream of people who consisted of the majority of the train's passengers who were all getting off at the same stop. Once back at street level and back to relying on foot power we made our way through the hordes of people making their way in to the Gare du Nord. As we came to the Mercure we were safe in the knowledge that even though time was a limited commodity we were OK; our reserves of the said commodity looked to be meeting our requirements with neither a shortfall, nor much surplus. Entering the Mercure we were met by the same concierge who quickly took our tags and retrieved our luggage for us. After enquiring briefly as to our enjoyment of the race and the atmosphere in the city during the afternoon he wished us a safe and speedy journey home and a polite goodbye. As we stepped back out on to the street I heard some familiar voices call out to me, "Hey pannier man!" Looking down the street we saw some of our fellow cyclists who had made the journey to the Gare du Nord with such a surplus of time on their hands that they had stopped for a farewell drink sitting in the late afternoon sunshine outside a bar a little way down the street from the station. Walking over to meet them we exchanged pleasantries and thoughts of the day before making our way en masse to the station.

Walking into the station, it looked to be in chaos with people running for trains to all sorts of destinations. Quickly we found our meeting point and were glad to see a lot of our peers, thankfully it was not long till Abrar and Ajay also arrived, and the closer it got to our deadline the more familiar faces appeared until everyone who was meant to be there had successfully made it. Being guided upstairs by our support staff and staff of the station we joined an orderly queue which split at the front and shuffled on towards two small grey boxes with turnstiles next to them. This, it turned out, was the French border control; as I got up close to the front of my queue I realised the other part of the queue was made up of random individuals not part of our cycling journey who happened to be boarding the same Eurostar departure as we were. Never being one to be silent in the presence of a group of people I don't know I began to engage anyone and everyone in short conversations and enquire how each of them got there. One group of four lads who looked vaguely bohemian or of a laid back hippy nature were heavily loaded with sleeping bags and an old ex-military type of tent. Having recently finished university together they had taken a leisurely cycling holiday through northern France in time to catch a couple of stages of the TDF and were now on their way home. Upon hearing that they had planned their own route and had only covered some forty miles a day over five days, camping overnight wherever they could, I found myself making mental notes and ideas of how to go about convincing Rosie to overcome her distain for cycling so that we could enjoy our mutual love of camping and have a romantic getaway recreating their slow and gentle journey. I quickly came to the conclusion that I stood more hope of convincing her to let me join the AMR London to Paris 2012 and meeting me at the finish line, and I shelved the idea of a cycling holiday. Turning the topic of conversation from themselves to me, the graduates enquired as to my story. Giving them the quick rundown of much of what I have discussed in the pages of this book, I found that they were left in shock upon the revelation that from a similar starting point and finishing point my journey had covered approximately twice the distance in the same time frame. By the time their minds had comprehended what I had told them it was time for me to bid them farewell as I was at the front of my queue and therefore called forward to the booth in front of me. Walking right up to the booth I expected similar scrutinising of my being as at airport security. To my shock and disbelief the person operating the booth was more laid back and quick to allow me through than the M4 tollbooth operators when driving into south Wales from England. Passing through the turnstile I had officially left France and now found myself at the back of the queue again, only this time for the British border control which was reassuringly rigorous and detailed in their scrutinizing of each member of the queue and their luggage before allowing them to pass through and go downstairs to the Eurostar platform, which was separated from the rest of the station by a large glass wall. As I boarded the Eurostar for the first time in my life I quickly began to realise that it was an anticlimactic feeling and a sense of being underwhelmed. I don't know if there is a class system on the Eurostar and therefore a far more plush cabin at one end or the other but the coaches we walked through finding our seats were no more or less comfortable or spacious than any of the standard class cross-country trains I had sat on when journeying to university from Rosie's student house in Exeter. With that said, the Eurostar and its domestic equivalents within the British Isles are more comfortable and spacious than the cramped uncomfortable seating and walkways aboard flights with budget airlines. Eventually finding my seat I spent a short while watching the French countryside whistle past the window until we began to sink into the ground, signifying that we were about to leave French soil and enter the Channel Tunnel. Realising that we were almost half way through our train journey and that I had not eaten for a couple of hours by this point I made my way through the train to the buffet car. This turned out to look far more like a train station cafe than the equivalent carriage aboard any domestic train I have ever been on in the UK. It had a long counter running down one wall with a couple of staff members and two tills at one end; across from this there were a number of high bar stools pushed partially under a shelf looking out of the windows with posters hanging on the walls at either end. There was a massive queue snaking round the room which I joined the back of and proceeded to wait my turn. The man directly in front of me was wearing an AMR cycling top but I did not recognise him as being from my route so I enquired which one he had been a part of. To this he replied that he was basically a major fan of professional cycling and was in near professional athlete fitness himself so had been involved in the 24-hour route which had covered the whole journey in one day all by only a marginally more direct route. As he told me this I began to feel in awe of him the way the graduates had been of me at the Eurostar terminal. The buffet car was so slow in processing people that I was able to engage him in an in-depth conversation about the riders and cycling teams he followed and cheered for during the professional events he watched before we both finally got served. I knew that I wanted to get rid of as much of my leftover Euros as possible and so was planning to buy something large and filling to eat and a bottle of water to drink but was disappointed by the very slim options left available. I finally settled on a massively overpriced beef burger that tasted substance-less and nutritionally void in exactly the same over-microwaved trashy way as the ones I described during my rant about train station food outlets earlier. Only this time even more ridiculously overpriced, costing me almost as much as a two course meal at one of my favourite pizzerias (Settantanove, Ilfracombe high street). Leaving the buffet car it became apparent that I had been queuing so long that by the time I returned to my seat we were almost reaching the outskirts of London and almost at the end of our international train ride. Soon enough we pulled in to the international terminal at Kings Cross St Pancras train station. It was a large and quite beautiful building of predominantly Victorian red brick architecture with a massive arched glass roof high above covering the platforms. Stepping off the train I took a glance at my mobile phone to check the time, it was 22:38 in the evening so I sent Rosie and my family text messages to say I had safely returned to the country. The station was a ghost town with the only movement seeming to be my fellow Eurostar passengers disembarking. Bidding each other farewell, we split up and ventured off on our individual homeward journeys. Under instruction from the support team I made my way out of the building to collect my bike from the designated collection point. Moments after I received a text from Rosie to say that Bonnie had parked down by the taxi drop off, was looking for me and had been given my phone number just in case she couldn't find me. It didn't take long before she flung her arms around me and gave me a hug in a sister-in-law kind of way. With my little suitcase in one hand and my bike on the opposite shoulder I followed Bonnie out to her little hatchback run-around and loaded it in the best I could. This seemed far more difficult a task than I knew it should have been but eventually we were on our way. Thanking her for picking me up and for putting me up for the night, I explained to Bonnie some of the humorous moments of the journey, how I wanted to take on another such journey as soon as was possible and eventually how I wanted to take her sister with me in future. Arriving at her home in a suburb of south London Bonnie helped me in with my bike and baggage and offered me a drink and a bite to eat. We stood in the kitchen chatting with her husband to be Euan, Euan was a man I enjoyed the company of on the few instances we had met at occasions such as Christmas and New Year celebrations. Standing roughly an inch taller than me, weighing in slightly less but at a similar mass, we shared the same hair colour and style at the time causing Euan and I to look surprisingly similar for two people from opposite ends of the British Isles. Whereas my roots are planted firmly in the south western corner of England, Euan's heritage was that of the highlands of Scotland. When out in public it had previously been quite a point of ridicule and jest by third parties how two beautiful sisters who looked incredibly similar had gone their separate ways in life, only to find men who looked as though they could have been related. Euan was an ex-professional snowboarder involved in television broadcasting of sporting events since returning to the UK after a number of years in the mountains of the south of France. There was a near identical age gap between Euan and Bonnie as there was between Rosie and me, with Euan being some four years more senior than Bonnie, who in turn was a year and a half senior to me and six years older than her little sister Rosie. Being that he was a big sports fan with both personal and professional interest Euan was keen to hear all about my journey and my experience of the TDF and so I again recounted my story until the clock struck 12:30 a.m. and we all decided it was time to call in a night. Bonnie and Euan showed me to their spare room and explained where the bathroom and toilet were before going upstairs to bed leaving me to get comfortable and settled in for the night.

Chapter Twenty-Three

Day Six and Beyond: My Return to Home Life

I awoke on the 25th of July in the early morning dazed and a little confused, feeling as if was still on a cycling challenge and that the room I woke in I didn't recognise as my own because it was just another hotel room. Snapping back to reality as my mind recalled the events of the previous twenty-four hours I felt in emotional turmoil, both sad not to have woken up in a room with Harshal and eager to get back on the road home. Not wanting to wake Bonnie or Euan at too early an hour, I began moving round their house with the swift calm silence of a ninja, a skillset I had gained as a teenager which I used and further enhanced during my university days before I met Rosie, back when one by one I dated several women who lived in the same building. After I had washed, dressed and repacked my things I sat down to purchase train tickets from Paddington back to Barnstaple. It was at this point that Bonnie appeared and offered me a bacon sandwich for breakfast, and while we ate breakfast Bonnie and Euan enquired as to my travel arrangements. This resulted in them both giving me completely different routes through to

Paddington station that they jotted down on scraps of paper and sticky backed card. Walking down to their front door to collect my bike from its resting place by their hallway radiator I remembered the difficulty and extreme complication Bonnie and I had experienced loading my bike into her car. I felt that I had to sincerely apologise to her for the fact that in my tired and underfed state I had completely forgotten that with the pull of two small levers the wheels quickly disengage from the forks and become separated from the frame. A fact that would have made loading it in her hatchback that night far easier had I remembered. Bidding them farewell I thanked them for their hospitality and hoped to see them again soon. I left their home carrying the bike and my luggage down the road in the direction of their local train station. Around the corner I almost literally bumped in to a little, short man of whom I guessed was Iranian origin who seemed eager to hear my story and find out how I ended up with a bike with two flat tyres. Upon hearing my tale he told me it was a wonderful uplifting sentiment to see a man whose bike had carried him so far repaying the favour and carrying the bike home to fix it. Finding out that I was heading for the train station, the same as him, he offered to help me carry my load. At the station I thanked him for his help and kindness and as we parted ways I wished him good luck. The counter staff at the ticket office informed me that I would be unable to take my bike on the underground so would have to make other arrangements to get to Paddington, once I had travelled as far into the centre of the city as I could aboard the next overground train which terminated near the tower of London. He was able to also inform me of a bike shop near the Tower called "On Your Bike" and so I left my bike in their capable hands while I went off in search of some lunch. Ten minutes later and luckily before I had even decided on where to eat I received a phone call from my father who seemed a little confused and anxious to contact me, it turned out that I had made a minor error on the form I was required to fill in when dropping my bike off to be repaired. On the section of contact details I had put my home phone number which although correct was useless for the shop to use as I was still 180 miles as the crow flies away from home and should have given my mobile number as it was the shop who needed to speak to me and my father was passing the message on. After putting down the phone I jogged back to the shop to speak to their technician. He had replaced my wheel's faulty rim tape with the correct type and wished to know which price range or particular brand of tyre I wished to have fitted. After explaining to him the bike's average usage, the terrain most commonly travelled and that within the realms of what was reasonably practicable I had quite a large budget for tyres after witnessing what difference the correct type made to performance with both the bike and the rx-8, I was keen to have the best I could afford but was quite happy with the Bontragers I had borrowed in France. He agreed that they were the ideal option, and finally he enquired if I would be interested in him giving the whole bike a clean-up and setup check. I agreed to this on the grounds of a fixed price deal for the completion of the work and set an alarm on my phone to return an hour later to collect my chariot and headed off once again in search of the nearest pub to purchase some lunch.

Refuelled and reunited with my wheels I strapped my suitcase over the top of my pannier rack and proceeded to test out my newly refurbished vehicle by cycling around London, making my way to Paddington station. I can quite happily report that by use of the blue tarmacked cycle super highways, two wheels is a perfectly easy and rapid method of traversing the British capital without the need of hot, sweaty, over crowded tube trains or traffic jams. I arrived at Paddington with perfect timing to board a train bound for Plymouth which I knew would be making a stop at Exeter St David's. Once aboard and speeding out of the city I phoned my family to tell them of my approximate arrival time. Due to the apparent lateness of the hour in which I would have got home my parents instead dispatched Neil and his little red van to meet me at Tiverton Parkway train station. My journey across from London was long and seemingly uneventful since from London as far as Tiverton I was standing in the little corridor by one of the external carriage doors, trying to keep my bike from being an obstruction to people boarding or alighting the train. Once off the train and loaded in to Neil's van I had to endure the boring monotony that was the A361 north Devon link road yet again, only this time instead of being in control of my own vector and velocity behind the wheel of my preppy little Mini or my exciting rear-end happy RX-8, I was in the passenger seat of a underpowered little van with a nervous extremely risk averse driver. For this reason it took almost as long to get home as it would have using public transport. With all that said I was glad to be home and to be able to tell my family my story in detail, explaining almost hiring bikes at midnight and the bars we drank in. I quickly settled back in to my near perfect life and began finalising the details of my next academic undertaking; a Master's degree in Biomedical Science by distance learning as to remove the need for quite so much driving to and from my chosen establishment. I also began to look at the piles of notes I had regarding my experiences with different transport and how I was best going to compile this piece of literature, and finally I began planning my next training rides, wanting to immediately begin preparing my body for another challenge of even larger proportions, while trying almost completely unsuccessfully to inspire Rosie to join me on two wheels. A week passed and soon I was back on the bike leaving Rosie at home entertaining a couple of her school friends who had dropped in to visit her. It was the first day I had been able to get back on the road with two wheels since my day in London and I was itching to cover some distance and push myself. I decided not to use my usual training route, which travels through the villages of Georgeham, Croyde, Braunton, and the town of Barnstaple, which with its long sections of near flat road makes for an enjoyable ride. Instead I decided to cycle in the opposite direction along the coastal road from one side of Ilfracombe through the other then past Berrynarbor through Combe Martin, a village with one of the longest high streets in the country, which used to have an incredible pub to populous ratio of something like a pub for every twenty-seven people of its inhabitancy of six hundred. I ended my outward ride in the direction of Black Moorgate on the undulating hilly landscape at the edge of Exmoor National Park before turning back and returning home for dinner. This constituted a considerable increase in difficulty for my cycle training, going from a thirty mile round trip of mostly flat, unchallenging terrain interspaced with safe cycle paths and country roads, to winding country roads climbing steep gradients at punishingly regular intervals. Arriving at the car park which overlooks the beach at the entrance to Combe Martin I stopped for a moment to take on some water and send a multimedia picture message to Rosie as a time stamp to prove how far I had travelled since leaving the house, covering my first two gradients and a total of seven miles in a little under twenty-five minutes. Already I was feeling drained and reminiscent of the hills we conquered between London and Paris. Knowing how I had to dig deep and soldier on if I wanted to push myself to breaking point and build more muscle to make future climbs easier, I quickly got back on the bike and powered through Combe Martin past the homes of some of my school friends and out on to Exmoor in search of the next stamina destroying hill to test my resolve. Another twenty minutes passed and with my cycle computer reading a distance of eighteen miles I felt broken. At that point I knew it was time to turn back and make the return journey. This was undertaken at a slower more grinding pace as I felt my body straining to keep the bike in forward motion; I began to feel that I had made the wrong decision and should have taken my previous route one more time before undertaking a cycling tour of the west fringe of Exmoor. Especially due to my previous knowledge that some cars struggle with the terrain of the area. Finally I returned home physically broken, disappointed and dispirited by what was in my eyes an abject failure. My family consoled me and tried to raise my spirits with their kind words. The rest of the afternoon all I wanted was to sit on my own and critically analyse my performance while eating lots of steak and eggs in the hope that the proteins from the food would help repair and rebuild my burning muscles as I was determined to more successfully undertake the route again a few days later. Later that evening when Rosie and I went to bed cuddled up in our little flat with its massive bay windowed bedroom I reflected on my day in a more positive light, as for all my physical performance had been disappointing, it was simply a benchmark for me to later compare future performances against in the onward struggle to improve and better myself, firmly believing in the old sayings that Rome wasn't built in a day, and first-hand experience that a journey of over three hundred miles begins with a single step. I fell asleep that night safe in my own belief that my life was near perfect by my measure of happiness being defined as wanting what you have more so than having what you want. I drifted off to the land of dreams completely unaware and unafraid of what the future held. I was blissfully relaxed and unprepared for the oncoming morning of the 4th of August which brought with it the beginning of a horrific and devastatingly destructive long series of events which led to the near complete destruction of my whole world and the character you have been reading about throughout this book.

CPSIA information can be obtained
at www.ICGtesting.com
Printed in the USA
BVHW04s1952210618
519669BV00011B/101/P